Birmingham Royal Ballet

 Birmingham City Council

 Supported by ARTS COUNCIL ENGLAND

Birmingham Royal Ballet

Photography by Bill Cooper
Foreword and Chapter Introductions by David Bintley
Introduction by Judith Flanders

**BIRMINGHAM
ROYAL BALLET**

OBERON BOOKS
LONDON

First published in 2010 in the
United Kingdom by Oberon Books
in association with
Birmingham Royal Ballet

Oberon Books Ltd
521 Caledonian Road
London N7 9RH
info@oberonbooks.com
www.oberonbooks.com

Compiled by Kate Howells
and Lee Armstrong

Foreword and Chapter Introductions
copyright © David Bintley 2010

Introduction copyright
© Judith Flanders 2010

Production Photographs
copyright © Bill Cooper

Photograph of David Bintley
on page 6 copyright © Steve Hanson

A catalogue record for this book is
available from the British Library.

ISBN: 978-1-84943-097-5

Front cover: *E=mc²*: Elisha Willis and
Joseph Caley in 'Energy'
Endpapers: *Tombeaux*: Artists of
Birmingham Royal Ballet
Back cover: *E=mc²*: Artists of
Birmingham Royal Ballet in 'Celeritas²'

Design by Jeff Willis

Printed and bound in Great Britain by
CPI Antony Rowe, Chippenham.

CONTENTS

David Bintley
Photograph: Steve Hanson

FOREWORD

In 1990, Sadler's Wells Royal Ballet took an important step in its illustrious history, accepting the invitation from Birmingham City Council and Birmingham Hippodrome to become resident at the theatre in Hurst Street. The press described it at the time as 'the arts coup of the decade' and, 20 years on, we are delighted to be celebrating the intervening years and looking forward to the next 20 with this splendid book of performance pictures by Bill Cooper that capture the many faces and talents that have peopled the Company in that time, and the many ballets that we have performed.

There are many who were committed and worked hard to make the move to Birmingham happen, but without the leadership of Peter Wright I do not believe we would have become the Company we are today. It was his courage and vision that spearheaded the move, and his hardwork and determination that established the Company in this great city over the first five years.

Since I succeeded Peter, the last 15 years have been a whirlwind of activity and adventure. The Company has blazed the name of Birmingham across South Africa, Japan, China, the USA and Hong Kong, created over 30 new ballets and won numerous major dance awards. All this, and we still found time to give an average of 130 performances annually in Birmingham and around Britain!

No story of the last 20 years would be complete without acknowledging the commitment of the City of Birmingham and its people to the Company. The City was behind the initial move, and has supported us financially and in nameless other ways ever since. The people of Birmingham and its surrounding towns and villages took us to their hearts from the start. Our audiences have always been as enthusiastic for our new works as for our heritage ballets and the full-length classics. Arts Council England has also played a vital part in our success; they supported the move to provide a centre of excellence outside the capital and they have continued to believe in our achievements.

And, of course, the last 20 years would not have been the success they have been without each and every one of the people who have worked for the Company and with the Company in that time. It is a privilege to have shared the first 20 years of our history with so many committed experts, with such a wide range of skills and knowledge. Each has played a vital part.

David Bintley, Director

The Two Pigeons: Nao Sakuma as the Young Girl and Robert Parker
as the Young Man

'Respect the past, herald the future, but concentrate on the present': so ran the artistic credo of the matriarch of British dance, Dame Ninette de Valois – or 'Madam' as she was respectfully referred to. So too might run the artistic credo of Birmingham Royal Ballet today, if anyone had the time – or the interest – for formulating credos. Instead, as a flourishing company, Birmingham Royal Ballet lets its work speak for itself, and what work it is. Now, having celebrated its 20th anniversary on 10 March 2010, with a Royal Gala, Birmingham Royal Ballet is entering its adult life, looking forward to a healthy and happy maturity.

This was not always a likely outcome, for the Company's beginnings were little short of miraculous. In 1926 Ninette de Valois, a 28-year-old Irishwoman who had danced with Diaghilev's Ballets Russes, set about making the proverbial bricks without straw when she decided to single-handedly create British ballet. To this end she opened her grandly entitled Academy of Choregraphic [sic] Art in Kensington. When students failed to beat a path to her door, she began to teach movement to the actors at Lilian Baylis' Old Vic Theatre company, and there created *Les Petits Riens*, her first ballet, two years later. (David Bintley would pay homage to her in 1991 with his version of *Les Petits Riens*, created for The Royal Ballet School.) In 1931, Baylis added the rundown Sadler's Wells as an outpost to her Old Vic fiefdom, and there Madam set up first the Sadler's Wells Theatre School, then the Vic-Wells Ballet. In 1946, the first tiny shoots of what would ultimately flower into Birmingham Royal Ballet appeared, when Sadler's Wells Ballet decamped to the Royal Opera House (becoming The Royal Ballet in 1956); remaining behind, the various precursors of Birmingham Royal Ballet came in quick succession: Sadler's Wells Opera Ballet, Sadler's Wells Theatre Ballet, and then, for a long time, Sadler's Wells Royal Ballet.

For these companies Madam created works of her own – among them, *Job*, *The Rake's Progress*, *Checkmate* and *The Prospect Before Us* – and her great discovery Frederick Ashton created *Façade*, *Les Rendezvous*, *Les Patineurs* and *The Two Pigeons*; the great 19th-century classics were also staged, and all would ultimately find a home in Birmingham Royal Ballet's repertoire half a century later. In 1949, a young dancer named Peter Wright joined the Company, becoming ballet-master in 1955, and choreographing his first ballet (for the Royal Ballet) in 1957. Then came harder times, when the purpose of the Company seemed less clear: Sadler's Wells Ballet, renamed first the Royal Ballet Touring Company, and then the Royal Ballet New Group, left Sadler's Wells. Peter Wright became director in 1970, and although the focus was on new and experimental work, Wright's fine eye for productions ensured that the repertory was as broad as possible, while the Company's former music director, Barry Wordsworth, helped forge an exemplary musical path. Despite this, the Company's homelessness was unsustainable, and the New Group returned to the Wells, becoming Sadler's Wells Royal Ballet in 1976.

That same year, a young dancer from the Royal Ballet School joined the Company: David Bintley. He soon attracted Madam's notice in a rehearsal of *Job*, and she marked him down as someone to watch. Her eye for talent, even aged 80, was still sure: in 1978 SWRB performed Bintley's first professional piece of choreography, *The Outsider* (in a way that later appeared prophetic, it premiered at Birmingham Hippodrome). New pieces now poured out in a seemingly endless stream, but at this stage it was as a character dancer of genius that Bintley was recognized – no one who saw his Petrushka will ever forget his heartbreaking portrayal of the sawdust puppet with the real heart, whose valiant spirit overcomes even death. By 1983, however, still in his prime as a dancer, Bintley was named SWRB's resident choreographer, moving to the 'big' company, The Royal Ballet, three years later.

In his absence, great things were happening to the Royal's little sister. In 1989, the announcement was made: SWRB was to leave its home of nearly half a century, and take to the road once more, this time not on tour, but to move permanently to Birmingham. As an earnest of the artistic seriousness of purpose of this new enterprise, the Royal Ballet Sinfonia was created especially to perform with what was now known as Birmingham Royal Ballet. And so they went. Peter Wright continued to direct the Company he had served so well. Never better than as a master-stager of the classics, he had already produced *Swan Lake* and *The Sleeping Beauty* for the Company, both with

designs by Philip Prowse. (These productions, think many, are still among the finest to be seen.) In 1990, Birmingham Royal Ballet's first year, Wright added a magical *Nutcracker* to their repertoire, with designs by John Macfarlane, in a production dedicated to the City of Birmingham, as acknowledgement and thanks for its support in welcoming – indeed, wooing – the Company to its new home.

This production, and the Company's opening programme – a new work from David Bintley, *Brahms Handel Variations*, a revival of Ashton's *Jazz Calendar*, and Balanchine's *Theme and Variations* – could both have used as their titles Madam's credo. The template was set: classics, new choreography, and works from the canon of British ballet. David Bintley had an intimate knowledge of all three: he had experienced the classics as a dancer; he had spent the previous decade creating works in a torrent of invention, and he, more than anyone, embraced his British ballet heritage. 'Ashton, de Valois are worth holding on to,' he says. 'My philosophy is the same as theirs. My way of feeling about theatre and music and dance is the same as theirs.' And indeed, whose work could be more English, creating ballets as he has featuring King Arthur and Edward II; or set in turn-of-the-century Salford; or based on Thomas Hardy's *Far from the Madding Crowd*, with Gabriel Oak, a shepherd who plays a flute – England as Arcadia personified. Even some of his plotless ballets vibrate with Englishness – who but David Bintley would, as in *'Still Life' at the Penguin Café*, create a morris-dancing flea?

Bintley has at his core the English tradition of theatrical and narrative dance, with an inheritance from Ashton in his liking for small beaten steps, precision in the upper body and nuanced characterization. In addition, however, he has a formidable musical education behind him: the child of piano teachers and jazz musicians, he himself played the double-bass and was a chorister, and in rehearsal he has been known to follow the score:

probably the only choreographer since Balanchine who has been able to do so. And from Balanchine, he has incorporated not only an intense musicality, but also his vertiginous speed of movement and daring. Barry Wordsworth sees this combination as essential to the successful transition that occurred in 1995, when Peter Wright decided it was time to step down from day-to-day management. 'It was a natural progression more than a change,' says Wordsworth. 'It was important to have someone steeped in the Royal Ballet traditions: a man of David's pedigree knew how to take the Company to another place gently.'

'To another place gently': in 1998, to celebrate Madam's 100th birthday, Bintley invited Jean Bedells, an original cast-member in de Valois' *The Prospect Before Us*, to help him re-stage this long-neglected piece. Bedells passed on what she remembered; more was reconstructed from photographs; and Bintley then choreographed links in the style of de Valois for the sections that were beyond recall. 'To another place gently': the next year was another centenary, this time of Birmingham Hippodrome itself; and the event was celebrated by plans to move yet again to another place gently, to preserve tradition through renewal, knocking down much of the old building and creating a new Hippodrome in its place.

In new works, too, Bintley constantly returned to this tradition for nourishment. *Cyrano*, not at first glance an 'English' work, in fact takes the conventions of 19th-century theatrical melodrama – an English genre *par excellence*. Its score, by Carl Davis, draws on the composer's fascination with silent film; and these genres are transformed through Bintley's choreographic poetry into a study of ballet's universal themes, love and loss. Indeed, in 2002, Bintley suggested that his choreography for *Concert Fantasy*, to Tchaikovsky, was an attempt to reconcile the two extremes of that composer's nature, 'the tempestuous romantic and the strict classicist'. One might suggest that it is the two sides of David Bintley's own nature, the grand austerity of ballet and the exuberance of theatre, that power his work.

The traditions handed down are not choreographic alone: they are drilled into each generation of dancers by a formidable array of those who learned from de Valois, who worked with Ashton, and Cranko, and MacMillan themselves. Desmond Kelly danced with the Royal from 1970, moved to SWRB in 1976, becoming the Company's ballet-master in 1978, its assistant director in 1990, and only retiring in 2008, after 38 years – although he immediately took up the post of artistic director of Elmhurst School for Dance, one of Birmingham Royal Ballet's two feeder-schools (the other remains the Royal Ballet School). Similarly, Marion Tait joined the touring company from the Royal Ballet School in 1968, becoming Birmingham Royal Ballet's ballet-mistress on her retirement from performing in 1995, where she remains today. Company régisseur Ronald Plaisted went back even further: he joined SWRB in 1948, performing with the Company until he became ballet-master and then régisseur at Birmingham Royal Ballet until 1997. And the tradition continues: Michael O'Hare joined SWRB in 1980, and 30 years later is the Company's ballet-master. The Company's two other ballet-masters, while not Royal Ballet School trained, have a long pedigree of performing as Principals within the Company. Wolfgang Stollwitzer danced with Birmingham Royal Ballet from 1996 to 2004, having formerly been a Principal with Stuttgart Ballet; he rejoined the Company as ballet-master in 2008. Dominic Antonucci danced with American Ballet Theatre before joining the Company as a Soloist in 1994; he became ballet-master in 2009.

With this formidable array of working memories, Birmingham Royal Ballet can keep its heritage alive, performing many Ashton, Cranko and MacMillan pieces that are overlooked by other companies – in its most recent seasons, for example, the Company has performed MacMillan's *Romeo and Juliet*, *Elite Syncopations*, and *Concerto*; Ashton's *Two Pigeons*, *Enigma Variations* and *The Dream*; Cranko's *Brouillards*. Peter Wright's productions of *Swan Lake*, *The Nutcracker* and *The Sleeping Beauty* also keep audiences riveted, as do Nureyev's staging of *Raymonda Act III*, and Fokine's *The Firebird* and *Petrushka*; and that is before the new works and 20th-century re-stagings are counted – eight Bintley works, one by Hans van Manen, one by Stanton Welch, one by Garry Stewart, and four by Balanchine. 'Our dancers like to move differently,' says Bintley, with some understatement.

A risk for a company with such a prolific choreographer at its helm is that his work can take over, but Birmingham Royal Ballet is a company of many choreographic visions, not one. Choreographers know this, and jump at the chance to work with the Company. Even the Balanchine Trust, notoriously picky about which companies they will allow to perform which work, says, 'Birmingham Royal Ballet can have whatever [ballet] they want whenever they want it.' It is that simple: 'There are some companies we trust, and Birmingham Royal Ballet is one of them.' Similarly, Birmingham Royal Ballet's production of Jerome Robbins' *The Cage* in 1995/6 was the first time any company apart from the New York City Ballet had been permitted to stage this trail-blazing piece.

Bintley thinks that it is the long-term link between choreographer and dancer that makes his work possible: 'If you're a choreographer and your work isn't in the repertory, you have no influence over the way dancers do anything. The way I work here influences the way they dance everything else.' This suits his temperament: 'I'm not by nature a gypsy. I don't like landing in a company for six weeks, dumping something on them and leaving. I want to have a family – and familiarity – and have what I do seen in context.'

Although Bintley might not be a gypsy, his home is still a gypsy company. For much of its life SWRB was a touring group, and Birmingham Royal Ballet continues to have touring at its heart. It has become embedded in community life in Birmingham in a remarkably short space of time, but it is also embedded in many other communities across Britain as well. Touring at the core of its purpose makes for a small, tight company. There are no surplus dancers, no complete second casts, which ensures that everyone is ready to go, all the time: there are no routine performances. In 2004, the Arts Council helped fund a new initiative to enable the Company to tour to places it had never been before. Now instead of one large tour, the Company was split in two, to enable it to perform in towns with smaller venues, which previously had not been able to welcome the larger company. Two groups of approximately 30 dancers and 15 musicians each, with backstage and technical crews, took their standard repertory – no talking down, no patronizing the regions for Birmingham Royal Ballet – including Balanchine's *Concerto Barocco*, Ashton's *Monotones* and *Dante Sonata*, and MacMillan's *Elite Syncopations*. Then the Company joined up again to tour a more traditional venue – the Metropolitan Opera, in New York. This small/big, local/international pattern has just been repeated successfully in the 2009/10 season, with a national split tour and a trip to China.

Education and outreach sound phenomenally dull, but they are, together with a school, the essentials for any company: a school creates the dancers; education and outreach create the audiences who have faith in the dancers and their repertoire. Bintley is proud of Birmingham Royal Ballet's track record here: the Company has, he says, 'persuaded audiences that new work is not a high-risk thing', no easy feat, as many larger companies, endlessly dancing *Swan Lake* and *Romeo and Juliet* will agree.

Education is not an add-on for Birmingham Royal Ballet. By 1985, while still SWRB, the education department was up and running, with events across the country, and wherever the Company tours. The Company holds regular open rehearsals, classes (Company class, and also classes for Birmingham Royal Ballet's Friends), giving presentations on different aspects of the Company, workshops, pre-performance talks. All this ensures that communities everywhere feel that Birmingham Royal Ballet is their company, too.

Similarly, when touring internationally, collaborative projects are a matter of course, and an essential ingredient. In 2000, combined with its tour to Chicago, the Company established a link with Chicago's Gallery 37, which had over the years provided 20,000 young people with the opportunity to apprentice with professionals in various fields. With *'Still Life' at the Penguin Café* as their starting point, new technology enabled these two groups separated by some 4,000 miles to work collaboratively on a new piece, each in their own cities. The result was that in 2002 seven groups performed simultaneously in both cities, each broadcasting their sister-shows via live satellite link-ups. Community indeed.

Community work at home has been just as essential. From the beginning, there was a strong understanding from the City of Birmingham that Birmingham Royal Ballet would be a proud part of their city, and the Company has embraced this. What began as a requirement for funding, became, says Bintley, 'an essential part of our philosophy'. As far as he is concerned, working with children in particular is a joy: 'I like doing stuff with kids. At that age you remember some important person saying something to you, giving you a tip.' It means, he concludes simply, 'I can have an effect.' And no one can doubt Birmingham Royal Ballet's 20 years of effect.

Many projects work quietly, with little or no publicity apart from the enormous satisfaction gained by their participants and families. 'Freefall' is run with Fox Hollies School and Performing Arts College, where dancers with learning disabilities, disabled and abled dancers work together, producing their own choreography, staging productions, and, ultimately, gaining formal qualifications for their work. 'Dance Track', another long-term Birmingham project, provides free after-school dance classes for children who come from backgrounds where they might otherwise not be exposed to dance. The single qualification here is talent. By 2008, 30 schools in the Birmingham area were participating in spring workshops that are held annually for Year 1 pupils, where potential and aptitude are identified; these children attend dance classes for a year, then those who show further talent are encouraged to attend Elmhurst's Saturday Pre-Vocational Programme before applying to join the school at 11. From 2010, a formal link has been established with Elmhurst School for Dance, for children aged between five and 19.

Elmhurst has become a great feature of Birmingham and Birmingham Royal Ballet life. In 2004, the school relocated from Surrey, and became an important source for Birmingham Royal Ballet dancers. Only four years later, when Birmingham Town Hall was reopened by the Prince of Wales, Elmhurst School for Dance was a feature of the Gala evening, with participation from those Birmingham Royal Ballet dancers who had trained at the school.

Birmingham Royal Ballet's most high-profile education programme nationally has been 'Ballet Hoo!', the end result of which was televised in 2007. The plan was to work with a group of disadvantaged 15–20-year-olds for 18 months, together staging MacMillan's *Romeo and Juliet*. Desmond Kelly agreed to direct the production, with Marion Tait. She says that when she first started to dance, education 'wasn't looked on as a career move', but once she experienced what education means – changing people's lives, 'both theirs and ours', then magic happens: 'I still get a shiver talking about it.' 'Ballet Hoo!' came out of long years of similar projects. Says Bintley, 'This did not fall into our laps. It came from years and years of this kind of working with groups – not as large as this, and not in front of TV cameras – but we had the confidence and the mechanism to do it.' 300 young people began; 120 completed the first phase; 62 performed on television, in front of a broadcast audience of 4.5 million viewers. As well as the technical skills acquired, and the life-skills – hard work, application, discipline, working with a group to achieve a goal – the participants earned the equivalent of two GCSEs or B Techs, and many have continued with further education since then.

Nor are adults and the wider community overlooked: in conjunction with Bintley's *Arthur* ballets, the 'Living the Legend' project has seen the Birmingham Royal Ballet education department and six community dance groups, together with a performance group from DanceXchange, the dance agency for Birmingham and the West Midlands, use Arthurian legends to create their own show, with 80 dancers, and with new music created especially for them.

There are also professional programmes: Birmingham Royal Ballet is in partnership with Birmingham City University, enabling its theatre-design students to work with Birmingham Royal Ballet's technical department to acquire hands-on experience; similarly, Trinity College, London, runs course in Music Education, with input from musicians from the Royal Ballet Sinfonia, and they, together with Birmingham City University are also linked with the Pianists for Dance programme, run with Birmingham Conservatoire.

Birmingham Royal Ballet is not hubristic: it does not feel it is only the teacher. On the contrary, it knows how short dancers' careers are, and how much they need to prepare for a second life after performance. In 1997 the Company and the University of Birmingham established a degree course in Applied Dance in Education and the Community. Originally a two-year BPhil for professional dancers, such was its success that, by the time the first seven students were ready to graduate, it had become a three-year MA programme, and 11 more dancers were already enrolled for the next course.

Many of these educational programmes highlight music as much as dance, and that is no accident. The Royal Ballet Sinfonia, Birmingham Royal Ballet's own dedicated orchestra, is the only specialist ballet orchestra in Britain. For logistical reasons, it remains based in London. Birmingham Royal Ballet only needs it 35 weeks a year: this means that the musicians rely on London freelance work or teaching contracts for the remaining 18 weeks of the year. But nonetheless, the Sinfonia is a Birmingham institution, performing at Symphony Hall Birmingham as well as with Birmingham Royal Ballet, both at home and on tour. They also perform in concert venues in London, and are many foreign dance companies' orchestra of choice when they come to the UK. Birmingham Royal Ballet, with its vast and eclectic repertoire is possibly the only British company that could support a specialist orchestra: this is not *Swan Lake*, banged out 25 weeks of the year, but a full repertoire of 19th and 20th-century classics, as well as – that dream of all musicians – new music.

Barry Wordsworth thinks that working with a new score is 'the buzziest thing', and he remains especially proud of Birmingham Royal Ballet's record in commissioning new music. 'If you think back to the early days of the Royal Ballet, with de Valois and Constant Lambert [the Company's first music director] – it was Vaughan Williams, Arthur Bliss, Gavin Gordon, Geoffrey Toye, William Walton [whom they were using] – all British [composers], all making theatre music, telling stories, which is what the British are really good at.'

It is not merely the new compositions, however, that mark Birmingham Royal Ballet's dedication musically. Most touring companies today rely on pre-recorded music, which in Wordsworth's view – and in the view of most audiences – has a devastating impact on performance. 'If you rehearse or perform to a tape,' he says, 'you are always moving at the same speed, and it's all too easy for the dancers to stop listening, just letting their muscle memory take over. Then what you end up with is refined gymnastics, not dance.' Dance relies on change, on growth. Without changing and developing musical performances, dance is stifled; no one appreciates this more than Birmingham Royal Ballet – or perhaps that is no one except the audiences, who know that the Sinfonia is an equal partner in this artistic collaboration.

From 2005 to 2009, the Sinfonia and Birmingham Royal Ballet joined with the City of Birmingham Symphony and Chorus and with the Birmingham Contemporary Music Group in a stunningly ambitious plan, dubbed by some 'IgorFest': to perform in the city all Stravinsky's works over four years. As well as the Sinfonia's concert contributions, Birmingham Royal Ballet jumped in with both feet, so to speak, contributing 15 Stravinsky ballets over the four years, with four works new to the repertoire, and another four world premieres, including *Pulcinella*, the Company's first work by choreographer Kim Brandstrup; Michael Corder's *Baiser de la fée*; and the Stravinsky Choreographic Project, 'Dynamic Dance', which featured choreographic contributions from some of the Company's own dancers, Kosuke Yamamoto, Samara Downs, Kit Holder, Aonghus Hoole, Jenny Murphy, Glyn Scott and Nathanael Skelton.

This heavy workload was amazing, since it was only in 2009 that the Birmingham Hippodrome got its new state-of-the-art sprung floor, a technically innovative floated wood stage that has become a major component in keeping dancers as injury-free as possible. Even before that, though, the Company has been at the forefront of injury prevention for some time. In 2000-2001, as part of a major redevelopment of the theatre, Birmingham Royal Ballet's new Centre for the Prevention and Treatment of Dance Injuries was opened. It was the first in the country to have water-based training, and to incorporate preparation for new choreography by the creation of specific exercises to enable dancers' bodies to be ready for, and then recover from, unusual and original movement. The Centre serves Birmingham Royal Ballet, and also the greater West Midlands and the wider dance community. It is headed by Clinical Director Nick Allen, poached for the arts from Gloucester's Rugby Club, and the Centre is fully equipped for dance-based therapy – its pool is available not only for aerobic exercise and resistance work, but also for barre exercises: one side of the pool has a barre, just as in a studio, and therapists and dancers watch monitors to check correct positioning via an underwater camera.

With this kind of care for its dancers, and the astonishing variety and range of the repertoire, plus that dancers' dream, an in-house choreographer creating new works on them, Birmingham Royal Ballet's next 20 years looks rosy. Says Marion Tait, 'Every dancer who dances with Birmingham Royal Ballet feels there is a future. And a reason for a future, one that will develop, not stagnate. 20 years is reinforcing, a look to the future.' As she remembers now with a laugh, it was 'scary when we lost the financial stability' that came with SWRB's roles as the Royal Ballet's junior partner, but 'it seems to have gone OK!' Barry Wordsworth is less understated: the move was 'the best thing that ever happened to the Company; we retained all the benefits of the history and association, but on our own we could flower.'

Certainly the critics see a flowering. In this last season alone, Bintley's $E=mc^2$ brought rave reviews. Judith Mackrell, *The Guardian's* dance critic, thought the new piece was 'thrillingly constructed'. Even more importantly, she saw in it yet another step forward for Bintley, who has changed and grown so extraordinarily over the decades. It was, she said, like nothing he had ever produced.

Which bodes well for his next project. For many years, the Company had performed Peter Wright's glorious *Nutcracker* every Christmas. But Bintley is not simply a choreographer; he is a company administrator, and he feels it is good for neither audiences nor dancers to perform the same work over and over every year – the audiences drop away, and the dancers become jaded and give flat performances. So for Christmas 2003/4, he created *Beauty and the Beast*, an astonishingly dark and lovely production, with a new score by Glenn Buhr and breathtaking sets by Philip Prowse. Thus *The Nutcracker* could be 'rested', coming out fresh every second or third year, to newly invigorated audiences and performers. Now Bintley is planning another Christmas cracker: *Cinderella*.

At the time of writing he is, he says, 'right in the middle of it.' He will be using the familiar Prokofiev score; the designs will be by John Macfarlane, who designed Peter Wright's *Nutcracker*, and what has been seen so far is, says Bintley, quite simply 'stunning'. In fact, he jokes, the contribution of design and music is so good that his choreography will be redundant: 'All you need to do is just put the sets on the stage and turn on the music.' (Audiences might argue with that.) But Bintley sees his main challenge as breaking away from Ashton's version, known to so many generations of dance-watchers. He himself danced for many years in that production (his Ugly Stepsister was memorable). Now he has to create his own vision. It should not be a problem. As he says, 'I don't do anything these days that I haven't been thinking about for a long time. If it's still in my head 20 years later, it's worth doing.' *Cinderella*, clearly, has passed that test.

More good things are in train: the newly appointed music director joined the Company at the start of the 2010/11 season. Finding a replacement for Barry Wordsworth, who was intimately involved with the Company for 35 years, was not easy, but Koen Kessels sounds like the right man for the job. He was previously at the Théâtre de la Monnaie in Brussels, a hotbed of dance, from Béjart through Mark Morris and Anne Teresa de Keersmaeker, and he has also had a long association with the Royal Ballet of Flanders, conducting many 19th-century staples; furthermore,

he is a specialist in contemporary music, conducting for the Paris Opéra Ballet in both contemporary and classical works.

In 1996, when Bintley had only just taken over the directorship of Birmingham Royal Ballet, he said, 'Choreography has always been my main job. Directing is sort of easy as long as you've got ideas. It doesn't seem to be more than common sense.' At the time, that statement sounded like the unconsciously arrogant sentiment of youth – directing an easy job? But as the decades have rolled by, it seems that Bintley knew what he was talking about. Under his benign reign, Birmingham Royal Ballet has been allowed to flourish, taking in the best of new works, creating its own standards, and relying, ever and always, on its wonderful heritage, from Madam to Ashton, from Ashton to Wright, and then on to Bintley himself. Massine once said about Diaghilev's vision: 'It was a comet – it burnt everything it touched, and like all comets, it finally disappeared, leaving a train of stars.'

Madam's vision of a British dance heritage, Ashton's vision in turn, MacMillan's, what will one day be Bintley's, has also burnt like a comet, and from it, thrilled audiences everywhere can enjoy Birmingham Royal Ballet's train of stars, scattered in its wake.

Judith Flanders

The Nineteenth Century

1

The 19th-century ballets are the foundation stone of all modern ballet companies, and the techniques they employ are the grounding for all ballet dancers and choreographers. Birmingham Royal Ballet is truly fortunate to have a splendid array of productions of these great works, most of which were created for us by that master of the theatre, our Director Laureate, Sir Peter Wright.

David Bintley

Angela Paul, Carol-Anne Millar and Jenny Murphy (left to right, front row), with Artists of Birmingham Royal Ballet

Above: Nao Sakuma as Odette
Below: Jonathan Payn as Baron von Rothbart

Above: Nao Sakuma as Odile and Chi Cao as Prince Siegfried
Below: Nao Sakuma as Odile

Leticia Müller as Odette

Artists of Birmingham Royal Ballet

Rachel Hester as the Queen Mother, with Artists of Birmingham Royal Ballet

Carol-Anne Millar as a Courtesan

Left to right: Dianne Gray, Laura-Jane Gibson, Samara Downs, Viktoria
Walton, Céline Gittens, Arancha Baselga, Yvette Knight, Kristen McGarrity,
Callie Roberts, Carrie Johnson, Anniek Soobroy and Marion Rainer

Nao Sakuma and Chi Cao, with Artists of Birmingham Royal Ballet

Natasha Oughtred as Princess Aurora and Iain Mackay as Prince Florimund,
with Jenna Roberts as the Lilac Fairy and Artists of Birmingham Royal Ballet

Above: Susan Lucas in the *pas de quatre*

Below: Molly Smolen as the Fairy of Joy

Marion Tait as Carabosse, with Artists of Birmingham Royal Ballet

Above: Natasha Oughtred as Princess Aurora and Robert Parker as a Prince

Below: Leticia Müller as Princess Aurora and Annette Pain as the Queen, with Artists of Birmingham Royal Ballet

Samira Saidi as the Lilac Fairy

Lei Zhao as the Enchanted Princess

Above: Lei Zhao as the Enchanted Princess

Below: Ambra Vallo as the Enchanted Princess and Anthony King as the Bluebird

Nao Sakuma as Princess Aurora and Chi Cao as Prince Florimund

Monica Zamora as Giselle and Wolfgang Stollwitzer as Albrecht

Above left: Ambra Vallo as Giselle and Joseph Caley as Albrecht
Above right: Lei Zhao and Mathias Dingman in the 'Harvest *pas de deux*'
Below: Monica Zamora as Giselle, with Artists of Birmingham Royal Ballet

Above: Gaylene Cummerfield as Myrtha

Below left: Elisha Willis as Giselle and Jamie Bond as Albrecht

Leticia Müller as Giselle and Andrew Murphy as Albrecht

Above: Angela Paul, with Artists of Birmingham Royal Ballet as Wilis
Below: Leticia Müller as Giselle, with Artists of Birmingham Royal Ballet as Wilis

Michael O'Hare as Dr Coppélius, Rachel Peppin as Swanilda and Yi-Lei Cai as Franz

Coppélia

Above left: Ravenna Tucker as Swanilda and John Auld as Dr Coppélius

Above right: Elisha Willis as Swanilda and Iain Mackay as Franz

Below: Timothy Cross as Father Time, with Sonia Aguilar, Arancha Baselga, Candice Fotheringham, Virginia de Gersigny, Dianne Gray, Juliana Moraes, Jenny Murphy, Angela Paul, Lei Zhao, and students of the Royal Ballet School in 'The Dance of the Hours'

Elisha Willis as Raymonda and César Morales as Jean de Brienne, with Callie
Roberts, Aaron Robison, Natasha Oughtred, Jonathan Caguioa, Laura-Jane
Gibson, Jamie Bond, Nathanael Skelton, Sonia Aguilar, Joseph Caley,
Momoko Hirata, Mathias Dingman, Céline Gittens and Tyrone Singleton

Marion Tait as Mrs Stalhbaum, with Artists of Birmingham Royal Ballet

Lei Zhao as Clara and Dominic Antonucci as Drosselmeyer

Aaron Robison as King Rat

Above: Laëtitia Lo Sardo as Clara
Below: Jamie Bond as the Nutcracker Prince

Laëtitia Lo Sardo as Clara

Above left: Lei Zhao as Clara, with Nathanael Skelton, Oliver Till and James Grundy in the 'Russian Dance'

Below: Dianne Gray, Mathias Dingman and Richard Smith in the 'Spanish Dance'

Above right: Anniek Soobroy in the 'Waltz of the Flowers'

Christopher Larsen and Kit Holder in the 'Chinese Dance', with Lei Zhao as Clara

Above: (left to right) Nadia Frölich, Samara Downs, Jenny Murphy, Juliana Moraes, Arancha Baselga, Sonia Aguilar, Virginia de Gersigny, Anniek Soobroy, Josephine Pra and Silvia Jimenez in the 'Waltz of the Flowers'

Below right: Andrea Tredinnick in the 'Arabian Dance'

Gaylene Cummerfield as the Sugar Plum Fairy and Matthew Lawrence
as the Nutcracker Prince

Ballets
Russes

Diaghilev's Ballets Russes created what can only be described as a new 'Renaissance' in the world of art, when they roared out of Russia in 1909. An extraordinary convergence of exceptional artists in the fields of dance, music and design, resulted in an imaginative conflagration from which a host of seminal masterpieces resulted.

Our repertory includes a number of these exceptional pieces, many to the music of that great musical luminary of the 20th century, Igor Stravinsky.

David Bintley

Dominic Antonucci as the Moor, Elisha Willis as the Ballerina and
Alexander Campbell as Petrushka, with Artists of Birmingham Royal Ballet

Nao Sakuma as the Firebird and Iain Mackay as Ivan Tsarevich

Above: Valentin Olovyannikov as the Immortal Kostcheï, with Artists of Birmingham Royal Ballet

Below: Silvia Jimenez as the Beautiful Tsarevna and Iain Mackay as Ivan Tsarevich, with Artists of Birmingham Royal Ballet

Molly Smolen as the Chosen Maiden, with Veronique Tamaccio, Juliana Moraes
and Artists of Birmingham Royal Ballet as Maidens

Molly Smolen as the Chosen Maiden

Joseph Cipolla as the Miller

Monica Zamora as the Miller's Wife and David Morse as the Governor

Louise Britain, Jessica Clarke, Lisa Conway, Elizabeth Gray,
Simone Halfpenny, Jillian Mackrill, Gillian McLauren, Reiko Muira,
Jane Sparks, Helen Tardent, Sarah Toner, Andrea Tredinnick, Karen
Waldie, Lisa Williams and Monica Zamora

Louise Britain, Michela Centin, Simone Halfpenny, Jillian Mackrill,
Gillian McLauren, Elizabeth Otter, Mikaela Polley, Samira Saidi,
Melanie Soloman, Jane Sparks, Sarah Toner and Andrea Tredinnick,
with Artists of Birmingham Royal Ballet

Robert Parker as Apollo

Above: Elisha Willis as Terpsichore, Iain Mackay as Apollo and Nao Sakuma as Polyhymnia

Below: Nao Sakuma as Polyhymnia

Michael O'Hare as the Prodigal Son, with Artists of Birmingham Royal Ballet as the Drinking Companions

Above: Robert Parker as the Prodigal Son
Below: Michael O'Hare as the Prodigal Son

Heritage
Ballets

As one of the two Royal Ballet companies, the British ballet tradition is a core part of our being. Ninette de Valois, surely one of the greatest figures in dance history, spearheaded the establishment of a ballet company in London in the 1930s, and was the figurehead of the two Royal Ballet companies and their school until her death in 2001.

To me she was an ever-present mentor and, alongside her first company choreographer, Frederick Ashton, a deep source of inspiration. This section features some of the works created by the first and second generation of great choreographers to grow from within the Royal Ballet companies.

David Bintley

Michael O'Hare as Satan

Above left: Kevin O'Hare as Elihu

Below: Michael O'Hare as Satan, with Artists of Birmingham Royal Ballet as the Three Pestilences

Above right: Alain Dubreuil as Job and Michael O'Hare as Satan, with Artists of Birmingham Royal Ballet

David Justin as Monsieur Vestris

Rachel Peppin as Mademoiselle Théodore, Karina Hernandez as Cupid,
Michael O'Hare as Mr O'Reilly, Joseph Cipolla as Monsieur Didelot and
David Justin as Monsieur Vestris, with Artists of Birmingham Royal Ballet

David Bintley as the Red King and June Highwood as the Black Queen,
with Artists of the then Sadler's Wells Royal Ballet

Gaylene Cummerfield as the Gypsy Girl and Chi Cao as the Young Man

Above: Nao Sakuma as the Young Girl and Robert Parker as the Young Man

Below left: Robert Parker as the Young Man

Kosuke Yamamoto as the Gypsy Boy

Dante Sonata

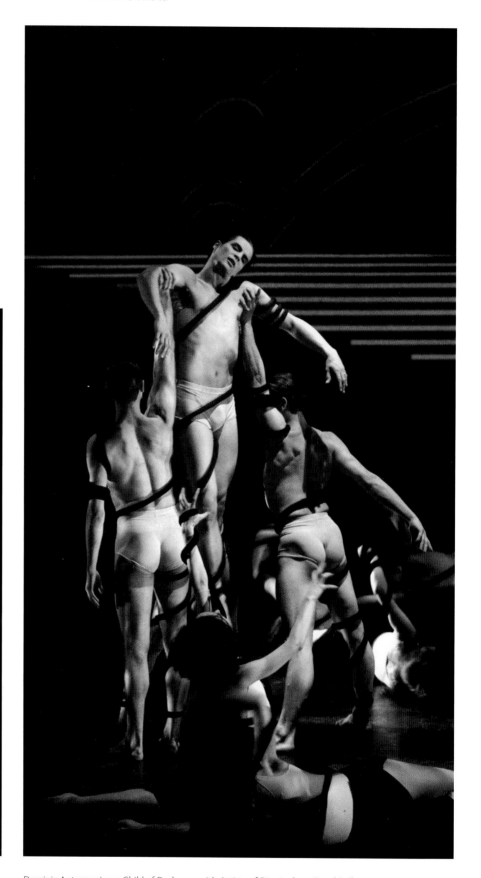

Silvia Jimenez and Toby Norman-Wright as
Children of Darkness

Dominic Antonucci as a Child of Darkness, with Artists of Birmingham Royal Ballet

Sherilyn Kennedy as the Lady and Desmond Kelly as Edward Elgar

Above: Kevin O'Hare as Arthur Troyte Griffith

Middle: Sherilyn Kennedy as the Lady

Below: Michael O'Hare as Hew David Steuart Powell

Above: Sherilyn Kennedy as Lady Elgar and Desmond Kelly as Edward Elgar

Victoria Marr as Lady Mary Lygon

Below left: César Morales as Arthur Troyte Griffith

Laura-Jane Gibson and Christopher Rodgers-Wilson as the Sailor Girl and Boy, and Nicki Moffatt and Oliver Till as the Country Girl and Boy

Natasha Oughtred as Isabel Fitton and Matthew Lawrence as Richard P. Arnold

Elisha Willis as Chloë and Iain Mackay as Daphnis, with Christopher Larsen,
Jamie Bond, Steven Monteith, Jonathan Caguioa, Alexander Campbell and
Joseph Caley as Shepherds, and Laura Purkiss, Arancha Baselga, Viktoria Walton,
Samara Downs, Marion Rainer and Momoko Hirata as Shepherdesses

Tom Rogers as Pan and Andrea Tredinnick, Silvia Jimenez and Victoria Marr as his Nymphs

Robert Parker and Monica Zamora, with Artists of Birmingham Royal Ballet

Rachel Peppin as Titania and Andrew Murphy as Oberon

Yi-Lei Cai as Puck and Andrew Murphy as Oberon

James Grundy as Bottom

Alexander Campbell as Puck

Duncan de Gruchy, Ravenna Tucker and Gary Shuker in 'Wednesday'

Above: Kevin O'Hare and Sherilyn Kennedy in 'Friday'

Below: Annette Pain in 'Monday'

Above: Nao Sakuma as Lise and David Morse as Widow Simone

Below: Paul Bayes-Kitcher as the Cockerel

Elisha Willis as Lise and Michael O'Hare as Widow Simone, with Silvia Jimenez, Laëtitia Lo Sardo, Arancha Baselga, Victoria Marr, Virginia de Gersigny, Viktoria Walton, Marion Rainer and Andrea Tredinnick as Lise's friends

Above: Molly Smolen as Lise

Below: Elisha Willis as Lise and Iain Mackay as Colas

Above left: James Grundy as Alain

Below left: David Morse as Widow Simone, Timothy Cross as Alain and Ronald Plaisted as Thomas, with Artists of Birmingham Royal Ballet

Above right: Ronald Plaisted as Thomas and Timothy Cross as Alain

Below right: Christopher Larsen as Alain

La Fille mal gardée

Above: Artists of Birmingham Royal Ballet

Below left: Nao Sakuma as Lise

Elisha Willis as Lise, Iain Mackay as Colas and James Grundy as Alain

Iain Mackay as Colas

Above: Molly Smolen as Lise, Michael O'Hare as Widow Simone and Lee Fisher as Thomas

Below: Molly Smolen as Lise and Tiit Helimets as Colas with
(front row) Nao Sakuma, Angela Paul, Karina Hernandez, Silvia Jimenez, and
(back row) Isabel McMeekan, Mikaela Polley, Victoria Marr and Asya Verzhbinsky

Above: David Morse as Widow Simone with Silvia Jimenez, Isabel McMeekan, Asya Verzhbinsky and Victoria Marr as Lise's friends

Nao Sakuma as Lise and Robert Parker as Colas

Below: Elisha Willis as Lise and Michael O'Hare as Widow Simone

Molly Smolen

Left: (from top) Ambra Vallo as the Two of Diamonds and James Grundy as the King of Spades

Yasuo Atsuji, Christopher Larsen, Steven Monteith, Joseph Caley and Tyrone Singleton as the Two, Three, Four, Five and Six of Hearts

Elisha Willis as the Queen of Hearts with Mathias Dingman as the Ten of Clubs, Fergus Campbell as the Ten of Spades, Robert Gravenor as the Seven of Diamonds and Kit Holder as the Seven of Hearts

Bottom left and right: Jamie Bond as the Joker

Above: Dominic Antonucci as Captain Belaye, with Artists of Birmingham Royal Ballet

Below left: Viktoria Walton as Blanche and Dominic Antonucci as Captain Belaye

Carol-Anne Millar as Pineapple Poll, with Artists of Birmingham Royal Ballet

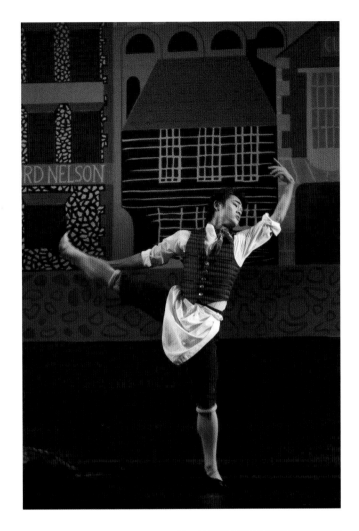

Above left: Kosuke Yamamoto as Jasper

Above and below right: Carol-Anne Millar as Pineapple Poll

Below left: Carol-Anne Millar as Pineapple Poll and Kosuke Yamamoto as Jasper

Ambra Vallo as La Capricciosa and James Grundy as Moondog

Jenna Roberts as the Girl

Richard Smith and Valentin Olovyannikov

Solitaire

Natasha Oughtred and Jamie Bond

Natasha Oughtred and Jamie Bond

Elite Syncopations

Above left: Miyako Yoshida in 'Stoptime Rag'   *Above right*: Jane Billson and Edwin Mota in 'The Alaskan Rag'

Below: Andrea Tredinnick and James Barton in
'The Alaskan Rag'

Above left: Carol-Anne Millar in 'Calliope Rag'

Middle left: Gaylene Cummerfield and Matthew Lawrence in 'Bethena Concert Waltz'

Above right: Rachel Peppin and Jamie Bond in 'The Golden Hours'

Middle right: Aaron Robison in 'Friday Night'

Below: (left to right) Aaron Robison, Valentin Olovyannikov, Dianne Gray, Andrea Tredinnick, Nathanael Skelton, Matthew Lawrence, Oliver Till, Gaylene Cummerfield, Carol-Anne Millar, James Barton, Richard Smith, Yasuo Atsuji and Sonia Aguilar in 'Cataract Rag'

Above: (left to right) Tyrone Singleton as Benvolio, Jamie Bond as Mercutio, Tiit Helimets as Romeo, David Morse as Lord Montague, Lei Zhao as Lady Montague, Michael O'Hare as Escalus, Samara Downs as Lady Capulet, Alain Dubreuil as Lord Capulet, Andy Rietschel as Tybalt, and Lee Fisher and Rory Mackay as Capulet Men

Chi Cao as Romeo

Above: Rachel Peppin as Juliet and Robert Parker as Romeo

David Morse as Friar Lawrence

Marion Tait as Juliet

Below left: Monica Zamora as Juliet

Ambra Vallo as Juliet and César Morales as Romeo

Jenna Roberts as Juliet

Jamie Bond as Mercutio

Above: Jamie Bond as Mercutio and Andy Rietschel as Tybalt
Below: Joseph Cipolla as Tybalt

Ambra Vallo as Juliet and Chi Cao as Romeo

International
Influences

4

Alongside the 19th-century classical repertory and the innovative works of the Ballets Russes, we are proud to also include, as a vital part of our own repertory, a broad range of works created for other companies around the world. These ballets include a large number of pieces by George Balanchine, one of my own particular ballet heroes, whose work spans much of the 20th century.

Throughout the 1990s the Company took part in 'Towards the Millennium', a review of the artistic output of each decade of the 20th century. As part of this Festival, the brainchild of Sir Simon Rattle, we brought into the repertory a number of ballets from the USA, including Antony Tudor's *Pillar of Fire*, Agnes de Mille's *Fall River Legend* and Jerome Robbins's *The Cage*. Add to those that giant of the 20th century, the Dutch choreographer Hans van Manen, and dance phenomenon Twyla Tharp, and the Company's repertoire assumes a distinctly international look.

David Bintley

Asta Bazeviciúte and Tiit Helimets, with Julie Comte, Angela Paul, Victoria
Marr and Juliana Moraes, and (behind) Arancha Baselga and Marion Rainer

Monica Zamora

Monica Zamora, Andrea Tredinnick and Joseph Cipolla

Gaylene Cummerfield, Natasha Oughtred, Ambra Vallo and Dominic Antonucci

Left and right: Monica Zamora and Joseph Cipolla

Symphony in Three Movements

Above: Andrea Tredinnick and Joseph Cipolla
Below: Artists of Birmingham Royal Ballet

Céline Gittens as the Striptease Girl and Robert Parker as the Hoofer

Above: Nao Sakuma, with students of Elmhurst School for Dance
Below: Chi Cao

Above: Simone Clarke, Asya Verzhbinsky, Dorcas Walters and Rachel Peppin
Below: Momoko Hirata

Left and right: Monica Zamora and Joseph Cipolla

Above: Victoria Marr as a Passer-by, with Michael Revie, Robert Parker and James Grundy as Sailors
Below: Rachel Peppin as a Passer-by and Robert Parker as a Sailor

Marion Tait as Lizzie Borden

Marion Tait as Hagar

Silvia Jimenez and Alexander Campbell in
'Somethin' Stupid' (choreography Twyla Tharp
© 1992)

Angela Paul and Robert Parker in 'That's Life'
(choreography Twyla Tharp © 1992)

Victoria Marr and Tyrone Singleton in 'One for
My Baby' (choreography Twyla Tharp © 1992)

Above: Nao Sakuma and Tiit Helimets (choreography
Twyla Tharp © 1992)

Below left: Ambra Vallo and Sergiu Pobereznic
(choreography Twyla Tharp © 1992)

Elisha Willis, Angela Paul, Carol-Anne Millar, Jonathan Payn, Robert Parker and James Grundy
(choreography Twyla Tharp © 1992)

Above: Samara Downs and Aaron Robison
Below: Robert Parker

Above: (left to right) Andrew Murphy, Asier Uriagereka, Dominic Antonucci, Ander Zabala, Anthony King, Jonathan Payn and Lee Fisher

Below: Isabel McMeekan, Dominic Antonucci and Asier Uriagereka

Leticia Müller

Above left: Catherine Batcheller and Kevin O'Hare
Above right: Samara Downs and Yasuo Atsuji
Below: Kevin O'Hare, Joseph Cipolla, Wolfgang Stollwitzer and Andrew Murphy

Created in Birmingham

5

Being part of the creative process is an invigorating experience for dancers. Guest choreographers offer the added advantage of a new perspective – a different dance style, an eye for spotting a particular talent in someone unexpected, a new dynamic that inspires a different level of performance and lifts everyone's game.

What can I say about the range of talented choreographers we have invited to create work on our dancers? That they come from places as far afield as the USA, Canada, Australia and Denmark, and that many of them are, or have been, Directors of their own companies, as well as award-winning choreographers and outstanding representatives of their various countries? What I can say, with certainty, is that Kim Brandstrup, Michael Corder, Oliver Hindle, James Kudelka, Garry Stewart, Stanton Welch and Lila York have each enriched and refreshed our repertory with their own varied styles and delighted both audiences and dancers alike with the uniqueness of their voices.

David Bintley

Above and below: Ambra Vallo as Pimpinella and Robert Parker as Pulcinella, with Artists of Birmingham Royal Ballet

Above: Ambra Vallo in 'Autumn'

Below: Ambra Vallo, Viktoria Walton, Kosuke Yamamoto, Robert Gravenor
and Feargus Campbell in 'Spring'

Above left: James Grundy in 'Autumn'
Above centre: Elisha Willis and Tiit Helimets in 'Summer'
Above right: Molly Smolen and Tiit Helimets in 'Winter'
Below: Chi Cao in 'Summer'

Dusty Button and Aaron Robison

Christopher Rodgers-Wilson

Above: (left to right) Victoria Marr, Samara Downs, Jonathan Caguioa, Aonghus Hoole, Joseph Caley, Nathanael Skelton, Laura Purkiss and Christopher Rodgers-Wilson

Below: Aonghus Hoole, Nathanael Skelton, Christopher Rodgers-Wilson, Robert Parker and Samara Downs

Joseph Caley

Above: Dorcas Walters

Below: Monica Zamora

Carol-Anne Millar

Jenna Roberts as the Fairy and Alexander Campbell as the Young Man, with
Artists of Birmingham Royal Ballet

Above: Natasha Oughtred as the Bride

Below: Jenna Roberts as the Fairy and Alexander Campbell as the Young Man, with Aonghus Hoole and Tom Rogers as Sprites

Dorcas Walters

Above: Robert Parker
Below: Leticia Müller

David Justin

Robert Parker

Sabrina Lenzi as the Ice Maiden

By the Company for the Company

One of the traditions of the Company I was determined to pursue, when I took over as Director, was that of encouraging dancers to explore their own choreographic talents. Over the years we have experimented with a number of ways of nurturing these aspirant choreographers and although the prime reason for doing so was to facilitate their own creative impulses, for many, the process shone a light on the whole choreographer/dancer relationship and gave them a greater insight into this vital creative partnership.

David Bintley

Elisha Willis and Robert Parker

Small Worlds

Left and right: Nao Sakuma and Chi Cao

Paramour

Left: David Yow, Andrea Tredinnick, Marion Tait, Gary Shucker, Kevin O'Hare, Gillian McLauren, Vincent Redmon and Andrew Wilson (original cast)

Unravelled, All for a Kiss and The End of Winter

Aaron Robison and Jonathan Caguioa in *Unravelled*

Above: Dianne Gray and Mathias Dingman in *All for a Kiss*
Below: Alexander Campbell in *The End of Winter*

Nao Sakuma and Alexander Campbell in *The End of Winter*

Monica Zamora and Duncan de Gruchy

Street

Jessica Clarke and Evan Williams

Mozart Mass in C minor

Artists of Birmingham Royal Ballet

Monica Zamora and Asier Uriagereka

Into the Ferment

Left: Virginia de Gersigny as a Girl, Rory Mackay as Willie, James Grundy as Rob and Tyrone Singleton as Alan

Above: Virginia de Gersigny as a Girl and Tyrone Singleton as Alan

Bright Young Things

Monica Zamora, with Artists of Birmingham Royal Ballet

Monica Zamora and Timothy Cross

Above left: Kosuke Yamamoto in 'Mercury'

Middle left: Juliana Moraes, Tyrone Singleton, Elisha Willis, Lei Zhao and James Grundy in 'Uranus'

Above right: Molly Smolen in 'Saturn'

Below: (left to right) Rory Mackay, Tom Rogers, Carrie Johnson, Anniek Soobroy, Ambra Vallo, Jamie Bond, Samara Downs, Aaron Robison, Dianne Gray and Jonathan Caguioa in 'Jupiter'

David Bintley

7

At the age of 16 I created my first ballet to Stravinsky's *The Soldier's Tale*. Made for my school friends and myself, it was the moment that I realized where my future and my real passion lay. Four years later, as a member of Sadler's Wells Royal Ballet, I made my first professional work, *The Outsider.*

From the very outset Dame Ninette de Valois gave me tremendous support, both as performer and choreographer, and I sincerely hope I have been true to Madam's vision, and that of her successors, Sir Frederick Ashton, Sir Kenneth MacMillan and Sir Peter Wright, in the works I have created for Birmingham.

As a dancer with Sadler's Wells Royal Ballet, it was Sir Peter who gave me my first choreographic opportunities with the Company and supported me through times both good and bad, never failing in his encouragement. It was a huge honour when I was appointed as his successor when he retired as Director of Birmingham Royal Ballet in 1995.

Inspiration for my ballets comes from diverse sources. Some are the result of a moment's epiphany, whilst many are developed from the kernel of an idea nurtured over many years. A slender theme, a story, a piece of music, even the arrival of a particular dancer can prove the catalyst for a new piece. And I am no less excited and challenged now than when I was that 16-year-old boy making his first ballet for his classmates!

David Bintley

Wolfgang Stollwitzer as Edward II and Andrew Murphy as Piers Gaveston

Above: Artists of Birmingham Royal Ballet
Below: Sabrina Lenzi as Queen Isabella, with Artists of Birmingham Royal Ballet

Leticia Müller as Queen Isabella

Kevin O'Hare as Edward II and Toby Norman-Wright as Lightborn

Elisha Willis as Queen Isabella and Iain Mackay as Edward II

Above: Kevin O'Hare as Edward II
Below: Joseph Cipolla as Mortimer

Above: (clockwise from front left) Angela Paul, Carol-Anne Millar, Viktoria Walton, Yvette Knight, Sonia Aguilar, Anniek Soobroy, Natasha Oughtred and Delia Mathews

Below: Natasha Oughtred and Kosuke Yamamoto

Delia Mathews and Tom Rogers

Nao Sakuma and Chi Cao

Leticia Müller as Bathsheba Everdene and Wolfgang Stollwitzer as Sergeant Francis Troy

Leticia Müller as Bathsheba Everdene and Michael O'Hare as Gabriel Oak

Leticia Müller as Bathsheba Everdene

Above: Simone Clarke, Dominic Antonucci and Andrew Murphy as Tumblers
Below: Leticia Müller as Bathsheba Everdene

Leticia Müller as Bathsheba Everdene and Joseph Cipolla as William Boldwood

Natasha Oughtred and Matthew Lawrence

David Justin

Above: Alexander Campbell
Below: Ambra Vallo and David Justin

Robert Parker as Arthur

Leticia Müller as Morgan Le Fay

Above: Joseph Cipolla as Merlin and David Justin as Uther Pendragon

Below left: Sabrina Lenzi as Igraine and Andrew Murphy as Lancelot

Leticia Müller as Morgan Le Fay

Wolfgang Stollwitzer as Arthur

Monica Zamora as Guinevere and Andrew Murphy as Lancelot

Above: David Justin as Uther Pendragon, with Toby Norman-Wright, Jonathan Payn, Robert Gravenor, Samuel Armstrong, Andrew Boddington, Christopher Larsen and Lee Fisher as the British Kings in *Arthur Part 1*

Below left: Ambra Vallo as Guinevere and Robert Parker as Mordred in *Arthur Part 2*

Below centre: Ambra Vallo as Guinevere and Andrew Murphy as Lancelot in *Arthur Part 2*

Wolfgang Stollwitzer as Arthur, Joseph Cipolla as Merlin and Robert Parker as Mordred in *Arthur Part 2*

Rachel Peppin as the Great Auk

Above: Rachel Peppin as the Great Auk

Below: Angela Paul as the Utah Longhorn Ram, with Robert Parker and Artists of Birmingham Royal Ballet

Robert Parker as the Texas Kangaroo Rat

Joseph Cipolla as the Southern Cape Zebra

Sandra Madgwick as Humboldt's Hog-Nosed Skunk Flea

Above: Silvia Jimenez and Yuri Zhukov as Rainforest People
Below: Toby Norman-Wright as the Brazilian Woolly Monkey

Ambra Vallo and Rachel Peppin (centre), with Artists of Birmingham Royal Ballet

Leticia Müller and Andrew Murphy

Chenca Williams as the Snow Queen, Vincent Redmon as Kay and Artists of Birmingham Royal Ballet

Above: Anna Villadolid as Gerda and Vincent Redmon as Kay
Below: Chenca Williams as the Snow Queen and Vincent Redmon as Kay

Above: Sabrina Lenzi and Kevin O'Hare
Below: Sabrina Lenzi, Kevin O'Hare and Chi Cao

Robert Parker as Hamlet, with Artists of Birmingham Royal Ballet

Above: Carol-Anne Millar as Kate and Krzysztof Nowogrodski as Petruchio

Below left: Ambra Vallo as Titania and James Grundy as Bottom

Robert Parker as Hamlet

The Shakespeare Suite

Above: (left to right) Jamie Bond as Romeo, Natasha Oughtred as Juliet, James Grundy as Bottom, Ambra Vallo as Titania, Carol-Anne Millar as Kate, Alexander Campbell as Hamlet, Silvia Jimenez as Lady Macbeth, Iain Mackay as Macbeth, Victoria Marr as Desdemona, Tyrone Singleton as Othello, Valentin Olovyannikov as Richard III and Angela Paul as Lady Anne, with Artists of Birmingham Royal Ballet

Below left: Leticia Müller as Juliet and Andrew Murphy as Romeo

Below centre: Wolfgang Stollwitzer as Macbeth

Below right: Angela Paul as Lady Anne and Valentin Olovyannikov as Richard III

Leticia Müller as Maggie Hobson and Desmond Kelly as Henry Hobson

Above: Artists of Birmingham Royal Ballet
Below: Leticia Müller as Maggie Hobson and Michael O'Hare as Will Mossop

Michael O'Hare as Will Mossop

Above: (left to right) Anne-Marie Little as Alice Hobson, Desmond Kelly as Henry Hobson, Anita Landa as
Mrs Hepworth, Michael O'Hare as Will Mossop, Leticia Müller as Maggie Hobson and Grace Maduell
as Vickey Hobson

Above: Rachel Hester as Vickey Hobson and James Grundy as Albert Prosser

Below: (left to right) Jamie Bond, Laura Purkiss, Andrea Tredinnick, Tyrone Singleton and Lei Zhao in 'Salvation Army'

Robert Parker in 'Annunciation'

Dorcas Walters, Robert Parker and David Justin in 'Transfiguration'

Above: Isabel McMeekan in 'The Protecting Veil'
Below: Ambra Vallo in 'Annunciation'

Above: Sabrina Lenzi and Tiit Helimets in
'Summer'

Below: Nao Sakuma in 'Spring'

Above: Andrew Murphy in 'Autumn'
Below: Momoko Hirata in 'Spring'

Below left: Robert Parker as the Beast and David Morse as the Merchant

Above and below right: Elisha Willis as Belle and Robert Parker as the Beast

Michael Revie as the Raven

Silvia Jimenez as Fière, Dominic Antonucci as Monsieur Cochon and Victoria Marr as Vanité

Above and below: Asta Bazeviciúte as Belle and Robert Parker as the Prince

Chi Cao as Qebhsnuf

Elisha Willis as Eurydice and Robert Parker as Orpheus

Above left: Elisha Willis as Eurydice and Robert Parker as Orpheus

Above right: Artists of Birmingham Royal Ballet as Furies

Below: Robert Parker as Orpheus and Tiit Helimets as Apollo, with Artists of Birmingham Royal Ballet

Dominic Antonucci as Aristaeus, with Samara Downs, Victoria Marr and Angela Paul as The Moisturisers

Robert Parker as Cyrano and Valentin Olovyannikov as Valvert

Robert Parker as Cyrano and Joseph Cipolla as the Comte de Guiche

Above: Chi Cao as Le Bret, with Artists of Birmingham Royal Ballet
Below: Robert Parker as Cyrano

Chi Cao as Le Bret, with Joseph Caley, Robert Gravenor, Tyrone Singleton, Kit Holder, Mathias Dingman, Rory Mackay, Steven Monteith and Jamie Bond as Cadets

Elisha Willis as Roxane and Robert Parker as Cyrano

Elisha Willis as Roxane, Chi Cao as Le Bret and Iain Mackay as Christian, with Nathanael Skelton,
Rory Mackay, Joseph Caley, Tyrone Singleton, Robert Gravenor, David Morse, Jamie Bond, Richard Smith,
James Barton, Mathias Dingman, Alexander Campbell, Kit Holder and Steven Monteith as Cadets

Elisha Willis as Roxane and Robert Parker
as Cyrano

Elisha Willis as Roxane and Iain Mackay as Christian

Above: Chenca Williams as the Floreadoress and Joseph Cipolla as the Floreador, with (clockwise from bottom left) Oksana Selezneva, Richard Whistler, Isabel McMeekan, Samuel Armstrong, Elizabeth Gray, Oliver Hindle, Louise Britain, Chi Cao and Rachel Hester

Below Left: Monica Zamora as Sugar Rum Cherry

Below right: Sandra Madgwick as Buttons, with Timothy Cross and Michael O'Hare as the Button Boys

Alexander Campbell as Eros and Chi Cao as Amynta

Nao Sakuma as Sylvia and Robert Parker as Orion

Above: Sabrina Lenzi as Volga Vouty

Below: (left to right) Chenca Williams as the Floreadoress, Joseph Cipolla as the Floreador, Monica Zamora as Sugar Rum Cherry, Andrea Tredinnick as Chinoiserie, Robert Parker as the Sailor, Dorcas Walters as Peanut Brittle, Silvia Jimenez as Candy Kane, David Justin as the Peanut Officer, Leticia Müller as Arabesque Cookie, Wolfgang Stollwitzer as Ivan and Sabrina Lenzi as Volga Vouty, with Artists of Birmingham Royal Ballet

Above: Molly Smolen and Tiit Helimets, with (left to right) Virginia de Gersigny, Jamie Bond, Viktoria Walton, Robert Gravenor, James Grundy, Lei Zhao, Kosuke Yamamoto, Angela Paul, and Artists of Birmingham Royal Ballet

Below: Virginia de Gersigny

Elisha Willis as Diana

Above: Elisha Willis as Diana
Below: Gaylene Cummerfield as Diana, with Artists of Birmingham Royal Ballet

Above and opposite: Nao Sakuma as Sylvia and Chi Cao as Amynta

Robert Parker in 'Take Five'

Above: Arancha Baselga, Anniek Soobroy and Kristen McGarrity in 'Three to Get Ready'

Middle: Joseph Caley in 'Four Square'

Below: Elisha Willis and Tyrone Singleton in 'Two Step'

Catherine Batcheller as Fortuna and Joseph Cipolla as the Third Seminarian

Above: Artists of Birmingham Royal Ballet as Seminarians
Below left: Sabrina Lenzi as Lover Girl and Michael O'Hare as the Second Seminarian

Leticia Müller as Roast Swan

Leticia Müller as Fortuna

Above: Leticia Müller as Fortuna and Iain Mackay as the Third Seminarian
Below: Victoria Marr as Fortuna, with Artists of Birmingham Royal Ballet

Gaylene Cummerfield, with Matthew Lawrence and Steven Monteith in 'Mass'

Above: Artists of Birmingham Royal Ballet in 'Mass'
Below left: Céline Gittens and Tom Rogers in 'Mass'

Samara Downs in 'The Manhattan Project'

BRB PRODUCTIONS
October 1990 – December 2010

KEY: BRB = Birmingham Royal Ballet; RBTC = Royal Ballet Touring Company; SWRB = Sadler's Wells Royal Ballet; SWTB = Sadler's Wells Theatre Ballet; SWB = Sadler's Wells Ballet; WP = World premiere; CP = Company premiere (first performance by Birmingham Royal Ballet). **Venues (UK)**: **Barnstaple** = Queens Theatre; **Bath** = Theatre Royal; **Belfast** = Grand Opera House; **Bham** = Birmingham Hippodrome; **Bham (Alex)** = Alexandra Theatre, Birmingham; **Bham (CF)** = Custard Factory, Birmingham; **Bham (Elm)** = Elmhurst School for Dance studio theatre; **Bham (NIA)** = National Indoor Arena, Birmingham; **Bham (Pat)** = Patrick Centre, Birmingham Hippodrome; **Bham (Rep)** = Birmingham Repertory Theatre; **Bham (SH)** = Symphony Hall, Birmingham; **Blenheim** = Blenheim Palace, Woodstock; **Brad** = Alhambra Theatre, Bradford; **Bristol** = Bristol Hippodrome; **Canterbury** = Marlowe Theatre; **Cardiff** = New Theatre; **Cardiff (WMC)** = Wales Millennium Centre; **Chelt** = Everyman Theatre, Cheltenham; **Cov** = Coventry Cathedral; **Durham** = Gala Theatre; **Ebourne** = Congress Theatre, Eastbourne; **Edin** = Edinburgh Festival Theatre; **Exeter** = Northcott Theatre; **Grimsby** = Auditorium; **Hereford** = New Hereford Theatre; **King's Lynn** = Corn Exchange; **Leeds** = Grand Theatre; **Lpool** = Empire Theatre, Liverpool; **Lon** = Sadler's Wells Theatre, London; **Lon (Bar)** = Barbican, London; **Lon (Col)** = London Coliseum; **Lon (Lyc)** = Lyceum Theatre, London; **Lon (ROH)** = Royal Opera House, Covent Garden; **Man** = Palace Theatre, Manchester; **Man (BW)** = Bridgewater Hall, Manchester; **Man (OH)** = Manchester Opera House; **Mbrough** = Middlesbrough Theatre; **Nhton** = Derngate Theatre, Northampton; **Oxford** = Apollo Theatre / New Theatre; **Plym** = Theatre Royal Plymouth; **Poole** = The Lighthouse; **Preston** = Guild Hall Centre; **Ross on Wye** = Pavilion Theatre; **Salfd** = The Lowry, Salford; **Sheff** = Lyceum Theatre, Sheffield; **Shton** = Mayflower Theatre, Southampton; **Stafford** = Gatehouse Theatre; **Sland** = Empire Theatre, Sunderland; **Telford** = Oakengates Theatre; **Truro** = Hall for Cornwall; **Yeovil** = Octagon Theatre; **York** = York Theatre Royal. **Venues (abroad)**: **Bangkok** = Thailand Cultural Centre, Bangkok, Thailand; **Beijing** = National Centre for the Performing Arts, Beijing, China; **Cape Town** = Nico Theatre Centre, Cape Town, South Africa; **Chicago** = Auditorium Theater, Chicago, USA; **Frankfurt** = Hoechst Jahrhunderthalle, Frankfurt, Germany; **Fukushima** = Fukushima-Ken Bunka Centre, Fukushima, Japan; **Guangzhou** = Baiyun International Convention Centre, Guangzhou, China; **Hamburg** = Staatsoper, Hamburg, Germany; **Hiroshima** = Hiroshima Yubin Chokin Hall, Japan; **Hong Kong** = Hong Kong Cultural Centre; **Hyogo** = Prefectural Hall, Hyogo, Japan; **Johannesburg** = Civic Theatre, Johannesburg, South Africa; **Kumamoto** = Kumamoto Shimin Kaikan, Kumamoto, Japan; **Kurashiki** = Kurashiki Shimin Kaikan, Kurashiki, Japan; **Kofu** = Yamanashi Kenmin Bunka Hall, Kofu, Japan; **Ludwigshafen** = Theatre im Pfalzbau, Luwigshafen, Germany; **Matsuyama** = Ehime Kenmin Bunka Kaikan, Matsuyama, Japan; **Nagoya** = Aichi Arts Centre, Nagoya, Japan; **New York** = Metropolitan Opera House, Lincoln Center; **New York (CC)** = City Center Theatre; **Numazu** = Numazu-shi Bunka Centre, Numazu, Japan; **Osaka** = Osaka Festival Hall, Osaka, Japan; **Pretoria** = State Theatre, Pretoria, South Africa; **Shanghai** = Grand Theatre, Shanghai, China; **Shiga** = Biwako Hall, Shiga, Japan; **Stuttgart** = Staatsoper, Stuttgart, Germany; **Tokyo** = Bunka Kaikan, Tokyo, Japan; **Tokyo (UP)** = U-Port Hall, Tokyo, Japan; **Turin** = Stagione d'opera, Turin, Italy; **Utsunomiya** = Tochigi-Ken Bunka Centre, Utsunomiya, Japan; **Virginia** = Chrysler Hall, Norfolk, Virginia, USA; **Yokohama** = Kanagawa Kenmin Hall, Yokohama, Japan

MAIN REPERTORY

Agon (Page 112)
Music Igor Stravinsky; *Choreography* George Balanchine © The George Balanchine Trust; *Staged by* Patricia Neary; *Lighting* Peter Teigen (from 2007). **WP:** 1 December 1957, New York City Ballet; **CP:** 28 February 1996, Bham. **Perf.** 1996: Bham, Lon (ROH), Plym, Sland; 1998: Cape Town, Johannesburg; 2007: Bham, Plym, Salfd, Sland

Airs
Music George Friedrich Handel; *Choreography* Paul Taylor; *Costumes* Gene Moore; *Lighting* Jennifer Tipton. **WP:** 1978, Paul Taylor Dance Company; **CP:** 10 May 1991. **Perf.** 1991: Bham, Lon, Shton

Allegri diversi
Music Gioacchino Rossini; *Choreography* David Bintley; *Designs* Terry Bartlett; *Lighting* John B. Read (Peter Teigen from 2010). **WP:** 15 January 1987, SWRB; **CP:** 20 April 2004, York. **Perf.** 2004: Durham, Mbrough, York; 2010: Durham, King's Lynn, Sheff, York

Apollo (Pages 60 & 61)
Music Igor Stravinsky; *Choreography* George Balanchine © The George Balanchine Trust; *Staged by* Richard Tanner; *Lighting* Peter Teigen. **WP:** originally titled *Apollon musagète*, 28 June 1928, Ballets Russes; **CP:** 24 September 2003, Bham. **Perf.** 2003: Bham, Plym, Sland; 2006: Bham, Exeter, Lon, Plym, Poole, Sland, Truro

Arthur Part 1 (Pages 164, 166, 168 & 169)
Music John McCabe; *Choreography* David Bintley; *Sets* Peter J. Davison; *Costumes* Jasper Conran; *Lighting* Peter Mumford; *Projections* Jon Driscoll (from 2001). **WP:** 25 January 2000, BRB, Bham. **Perf.** 2000: Bham, Brad, Lon (ROH), Plym, Sland; 2001: Lon, Plym, Salfd; 2003: Bham

Arthur Part 2 (Pages 165, 167 & 169)
Music John McCabe; *Choreography* David Bintley; *Sets* Peter J. Davison; *Costumes* Jasper Conran; *Lighting* Peter Mumford; *Projections* Jon Driscoll. **WP:** 9 May 2001, BRB, Lon. **Perf.** 2001: Lon, Plym, Salfd; 2003: Bham

Baiser de la fée, Le (Page 140)
Music Igor Stravinsky; *Choreography* James Kudelka; *Designs* Nadine Baylis; *Lighting* David A. Finn. **WP:** 26 September 1996, BRB, Bham. **Perf.** 1996: Bham, Bristol, Brad, Plym, Sland

Baiser de la fée, Le (Pages 136 & 137)
Music Igor Stravinsky; *Choreography* Michael Corder; *Designs* John F. Macfarlane; *Lighting* Paule Constable. **WP:** 3 July 2008, BRB, Bham. **Perf.** 2008: Bham, Cardiff, Edin, Lon

Beauty and the Beast (Pages 192-195)
Music Glenn Buhr; *Choreography* David Bintley; *Designs* Philip Prowse; *Lighting* Mark Jonathan.**WP:** 1 December 2003, BRB, Bham. **Perf.** 2003: Bham; 2004: Brad, Plym, Salfd, Sland; 2005: Bham; 2006: Hong Kong; 2008: Bham, Cardiff (WMC), Edin, Lon, Plym, Shiga, Sland, Tokyo; 2009: Beijing, Shanghai

Birthday Offering
Music Alexander Glazunov; *Choreography* Frederick Ashton; *Designs* Peter Farmer; *Lighting* Peter Mumford. **WP:** 5 May 1956, SWRB; **CP:** 27 September 1995, Bham. **Perf.** 1995: Bham, Bristol, Plym; 1996: Bham, Lpool, Lon (ROH), Plym, Shton, Sland

Brahms Handel Variations
Music Johannes Brahms; *Choreography* David Bintley; *Designs* Maria Djurkovic (Jasper Conran from 1994); *Lighting* John B. Read (Andy Phillips from 1994). **WP:** 30 October 1990, BRB, Bham. **Perf.** 1990: Bham; 1991: Cardiff, Lon (ROH), Plym, Sland; 1994: Bham, Bristol, Man

Bright Young Things (Page 147)
Music George Gershwin; *Choreography* Oliver Hindle; *Designs* David Blight; *Lighting* Paule Constable. **WP:** 29 May 1997, BRB, Bham. **Perf.** 1997: Bham, Lon (ROH), Plym

Brouillards
Music Claude Debussy; *Choreography* John Cranko; *Staged by* Jane Bourne; *Lighting* Nicholas Ware. **WP:** 8 March 1970, Würtemberg State Ballet; **CP:** 19 April 2005, Bath. **Perf.** 2005: Bath, Bham, Exeter, Truro, Yeovil; 2006: Durham, Grimsby, Sheff, York; 2010: Chelt, Poole, Truro

Burrow, The
Music Frank Martin; *Choreography and scenario* Kenneth MacMillan; *Designs* Nicholas Georgiadis; *Lighting* John B. Read. **WP:** 2 January 1958, RBTC; **CP:** 31 October 1991, Bham. **Perf.** 1991: Bham, Leeds; 1992: Brad, Canterbury, Ebourne, Lon

Cage, The (Page 117)
Music Igor Stravinsky; *Choreography* Jerome Robbins; *Staged by* Jean-Pierre Frohlich; *Sets* Jean Rosenthal; *Costumes* Ruth Sobatka; *Lighting* Perry Silvey. **WP:** 14 June 1951, New York City Ballet; **CP:** 28 February 1996, Bham. **Perf.** 1996: Bham, Brad, Plym, Sland

Card Game (Page 91)
Music Igor Stravinsky; *Choreography* John Cranko; *Scenario adapted by* John Cranko *from the original by* Igor Stravinsky *and* M. Malaieff; *Staged by* Georgette Tsinguirides; *Designs* Dorothée Zippel; *Lighting* William Bundy (Peter Teigen from 2008). **WP:** 22 January 1965, Stuttgart Ballet; **CP:** 6 March 1992, Bham. **Perf.** 1992: Bham, Bristol, Lon, Shton; 2008: Bham

Carmina burana (Pages 215-218)
Music Carl Orff; *Choreography* David Bintley; *Designs* Philip Prowse; *Lighting* Peter Mumford. **WP:** 27 September 1995, BRB, Bham. **Perf.** 1995: Bham, Bristol, Plym; 1996: Bham, Lpool, Lon (ROH), Shton; 1997: Lon (ROH), Man, Plym, Shton; 1998: Cape Town, Johannesburg; 2002: Bham, Edin; 2006: Bham, Plym

Centre and its Opposite, The (Pages 132 & 133)
Music Huey Benjamin; *Choreography* Garry Stewart; *Designs* Georg Meyer-Weil; *Lighting* Michael Mannion. **WP:** 12 May 2009, BRB, Chelt. **Perf.** 2009: Bham, Chelt, Exeter, Lon, Plym, Poole, Sland, Truro; 2010: Durham, King's Lynn, Sheff, York

Checkmate (Page 69)
Music Arthur Bliss; *Choreography* Ninette de Valois; *Designs* E. McKnight Kauffer; *Lighting* John B. Read. **WP:** 15 June 1937, Vic-Wells Ballet; **CP:** 5 October 2005, Bham. **Perf.** 2005: Bham, Edin, Lon, Plym, Sland

Choreartium (Pages 58 & 59)
Music Johannes Brahms; *Choreography* Léonide Massine; *Reconstruction and production* Tatiana Leskova; *Designs* Nadine Baylis; *Lighting* John B. Read. **WP:** 24 October 1933, Ballets Russes de Monte Carlo; **CP:** 25 October 1991, Bham. **Perf.** 1991: Bham, Leeds, Plym; 1992: Bristol, Shton; 1993: Bham, Brad, Lon (ROH); 1995: Bham, Brad, Ludwigshafen, Stuttgart

Choros (Page 178)
Music Aubrey Meyer; *Choreography* David Bintley; *Designs* Terry Bartlett; *Lighting* John B. Read. **WP:** 20 September 1983, SWRB; **CP:** 3 March 1999, Bham. **Perf.** 1999: Bham, Lpool

Cinderella
Music Sergei Prokofiev; *Choreography* David Bintley; *Designs* John F. Macfarlane; *Lighting* David A. Finn. **WP:** 24 November 2010, BRB, Bham. **Perf.** 2010: Bham

Concert Fantasy (Page 157)
Music Pyotr Ilyich Tchaikovsky; *Choreography* David Bintley; *Costume co-ordinator* Claire Leadbeater; *Lighting* Peter Teigen. **WP:** 2 October 2002, BRB, Bham. **Perf.** 2002: Bham, Plym, Sland; 2003: Brad, Edin, Salfd

Concerto (Pages 96 & 97)
Music Dmitri Shostakovich; *Choreography* Kenneth MacMillan; *Designs* Jürgen Rose; *Lighting* John B. Read (from 2008). **WP:** 30 November 1966, Deutsche Oper Ballett; **CP:** 11 June 1993, Bham. **Perf.** 1993: Bham, Brad, Lon (ROH), Shton; 2008: Bham; 2010: Bham, Lon, Plym

Concerto Barocco (Page 109)
Music Johann Sebastian Bach; *Choreography* George Balanchine © The George Balanchine Trust; *Staged by* Zippora Karz; *Lighting* Peter Teigen. **WP:** 29 May 1941, American Ballet Caravan; **CP:** 6 March 2001, Bham (Alex). **Perf.** 2001: Bham (Alex), Plym, Sland; 2004: Barnstaple, Bham Truro, Yeovil; 2008: Durham, King's Lynn, York

Coppélia (Pages 38 & 39)
Music Léo Delibes; *Choreography* Marius Petipa, Enrico Cecchetti *and* Peter Wright; *Production* Peter Wright; *Designs* Peter Farmer; *Lighting* John Hall (Peter Teigen from 2003). **WP:** 25 May 1870, Paris Opéra Ballet; **CP:** 3 March 1995, Bham. **Perf.** 1995: Bham, Brad, Lpool, Lon (ROH), Osaka, Plym, Shton, Sland, Tokyo; 1999: Bham, Plym, Sland; 2003: Bham, Brad, Edin, Plym, Salfd, Sland; 2007: Bham, Salfd; 2008: Hyogo, Tokyo (UP)

Cracked Nut, The
Charity celebrity version of Peter Wright's production of *The Nutcracker*. See *The Nutcracker* entry for details. **Perf.** 1998: Bham; 1999: Bham

Cyrano (Pages 200-205)
Music Carl Davis; *Choreography* David Bintley; *Designs* Hayden Griffin; *Lighting* Mark Jonathan; *Fight Director* Malcolm Ranson. **WP:** 7 February 2007, BRB, Bham. **Perf.** 2007: Bham, Oxford, Plym, Salfd, Sland; 2009: Belfast, Bham, Lon, Plym, Sland

Dance House, The (Pages 162 & 163)
Music Dmitri Shostakovich; *Choreography* David Bintley; *Designs* Robert Heindel; *Lighting* Lisa J. Pinkham. **WP:** 14 February 1995, San Francisco Ballet; **CP:** 13 May 1999, Bham. **Perf.** 1999: Bham, Plym, Sland; 2009: Bham, Durham, King's Lynn, Sheff, York; 2010: Chelt, Poole, Truro

Dante Sonata (Page 72)
Music Franz Liszt; *Arranged by* Constant Lambert; *Choreography* Frederick Ashton; *Staged by* Jean Bedells *and* Pauline Clayden *with assistance from* Pamela May; *Designs* Sophie Fedorovitch; *Lighting* Mark Jonathan. **WP:** 23 January 1940, SWB; **CP:** 14 April 2000, Bham (Rep). **Perf.** 2000: Bham (Rep), Brad, Plym, Sland; 2001: Lon; 2004: Bham, Durham, Mbrough, New York, York; 2005: Hamburg; 2008: Chelt, Exeter, Poole, Truro

Daphnis and Chloë (Pages 76 & 77)
Music Maurice Ravel; *Choreography* Frederick Ashton; *Designs* John Craxton; *Lighting* Peter Teigen. **WP:** 3 April 1951, SWTB; **CP:** 3 October 2007, Bham. **Perf.** 2007: Bham, Lon, Plym, Sland

Dark Horizons
Music Dmitri Shostakovich; *Arranged by* Rudolph Barshai; *Choreography* Oliver Hindle; *Designs* Peter Farley; *Lighting* John B. Read. **WP:** 24 March 1992, BRB, Lon. **Perf.** 1992: Bristol, Lon, Shton

Divertimento No.15
Music Wolfgang Amadeus Mozart; *Choreography* George Balanchine © The George Balanchine Trust; *Designs* Peter Farmer; *Staging* Victoria Simon; *Lighting* John Hall. **WP:** 31 May 1956, New York City Ballet; **CP:** 25 October 1991, Bham. **Perf.** 1991: Bham, Leeds; 1992: Lon

Dream, The (Pages 79-81)
Music Felix Mendelssohn; *Arranged by* John Lanchbery; *Choreography* Frederick Ashton; *Designs* Peter Farmer; *Lighting* John B. Read. **WP:** 2 April 1964, The Royal Ballet; **CP:** 3 November 1993, Bham. **Perf.** 1993: Bham, Plym; 1994: Brad, Ebourne, Lpool, Nhton, Sland; 1997: Bham, Brad, Lon (ROH), Man, Plym, Shton, Sland; 2009: Bham

Dumbarton Oaks (Page 143)
Music Igor Stravinsky; *Choreography and designs* Michael Kopinski; *Lighting* Peter Teigen. **WP:** 19 April 2005, BRB, Hull. **Perf.** 2005: Bham, Durham, Hull, Mbrough, York

Duo Concertante
Music Igor Stravinsky; *Choreography* Balanchine © The George Balanchine Trust; *Staged by* Eve Lawson; *Lighting* Ronald Bates. **WP:** 22 June 1972, New York City Ballet; **CP:** 19 April 2005, Hull. **Perf.** 2005: Bham, Durham, Hull, Mbrough, York

E=mc² (Pages 219, 220 & Covers)
Music Matthew Hindson; *Choreography* David Bintley; *Costumes* Kate Ford; *Lighting* Peter Mumford. **WP:** 23 September 2009, BRB, Bham. **Perf.** Bham, Lon, Plym, Sland

Edward II (Pages 151-155)
Music John McCabe; *Choreography* David Bintley; *Sets* Peter J. Davison; *Costumes* Jasper Conran; *Lighting* Peter Mumford **WP:** 15 April 1995, Stuttgart Ballet; **CP:** 9 October 1997, Bham. **Perf.** 1997: Bham, Brad, Bristol, Sland; 1998: Bham, Man, Plym; 1999: Lon; 2000: Hong Kong; 2001: New York (CC); 2007: Bham, Lon, Plym, Sland.

Elite Syncopations (Pages 98 & 99)
Music Scott Joplin and others; *Choreography* Kenneth MacMillan; *Designs* Ian Spurling. **WP:** 7 October 1974, The Royal Ballet; **CP:** 9 November 1990, Bham. **Perf.** 1990: Bham; 1992: Brad, Canterbury, Ebourne, Lon; 1993: Bham, Plym; 1994: Lon (ROH), Nhton; 1998: Bham, Brad, Bristol, Lpool, Man, Plym; 2004: Durham, Mbrough, York; 2005: Bath, Bham, Exeter, Truro, Yeovil; 2008: Chelt, Exeter, Poole, Truro; 2009: Durham, King's Lynn, Sheff, York

Enigma Variations (Pages 73-75)
Music Edward Elgar; *Choreography* Frederick Ashton; *Staged by* Michael Somes; *Designs* Julia Trevelyan Oman; *Lighting* William Bundy (Mark Jonathan from 2004). **WP:** 25 October 1968, The Royal Ballet; **CP:** 11 October 1994, Bham. **Perf.** 1994: Bham, Brad, Bristol, Edin, Plym; 1995: Bham, Ludwigshafen, Stuttgart; 2000: Bham (Rep), Brad, Plym, Sland; 2004: Bham, New York; 2005: Hamburg; 2009: Bham, Lon (Col), Plym, Salfd, Sland

Façade
Music William Walton; *Choreography* Frederick Ashton; *Designs* John Armstrong; *Lighting* Peter Teigen (from 2002). **WP:** 26 April 1931, Carmago Society; **CP:** 5 April 1991, Sland. **Perf.** 1991: Cardiff, Lon, Sland; 1993: Brad, Lon, Shton; 1995: Bham; 2002: Bham

Fall River Legend (Page 119)
Music Morton Gould; *Choreography* Agnes de Mille; *Staging* Terrence Orr; *Sets* Oliver Smith; *Costumes* Miles White; *Lighting* Thomas R. Skelton. **WP:** 22 April 1948, American Ballet Theatre; **CP:** 31 March 1994, Lon (ROH). **Perf.** 1994: Bham, Brad, Ebourne, Lon (ROH)

Fancy Free (Page 118)
Music Leonard Bernstein; *Choreography* Jerome Robbins; *Staged by* Jean-Pierre Frohlich; *Sets* Oliver Smith; *Costumes* Kermit Love; *Lighting* Jennifer Tipton. **WP:** 18 April 1944, Ballet Theatre; **CP:** 2 October 2002, Bham. **Perf.** 2002: Bham Plym, Sland; 2003: Brad, Edin, Salfd

Far from the Madding Crowd (Pages 158-161)
Music Paul Reade; *Choreography* David Bintley; *Designs* Hayden Griffin; *Lighting* Mark Jonathan. **WP:** 22 February 1996, BRB, Bham. **Perf.** 1996: Bham, Brad, Lpool, Lon (ROH), Plym, Shton, Sland; 1998: Bham, Brad, Bristol, Cape Town, Lpool, Pretoria; 2002: Bham, Plym, Sland

Fille mal gardée, La (Pages 84-89)
Music Ferdinand Hérold; *Freely adapted and arranged by* John Lanchbery; *Scenario* Jean Dauberval; *Choreography* Frederick Ashton; *Designs* Osbert Lancaster; *Lighting* Peter Teigen after the original design (from 2001). **WP:** 28 January 1960, The Royal Ballet; **CP:** 4 July 1991, Brad. **Perf.** 1991: Brad, Bristol, Lon (ROH); 1994: Bham, Brad, Bristol, Plym, Sland, Turin; 1995: Lon; 1996: Bham; 2001: Bham (Alex), Brad, Plym, Sland; 2004: Bham, Salfd; 2006: Bham, Cardiff (WMC), Salfd

Fin du jour, La
Music Maurice Ravel; *Choreography* Kenneth MacMillan; *Designs* Ian Spurling; *Lighting* John B. Read. **WP:** 15 March 1979, The Royal Ballet; **CP:** 9 November 1990, Bham. **Perf.** 1990: Bham; 1991: Man

Firebird, The (Pages 52 & 53)
Music Igor Stravinsky; *Choreography* Mikhail Fokine; *Designs* Natalia Goncharova; *Lighting* John B. Read. **WP:** 25 June 1910, Ballets Russes; **CP:** 3 May 2006, Bham. **Perf.** 2006: Bham, Lon, Plym, Sland; 2008: Bham, Cardiff (WMC), Edin, Lon

Five Brahms Waltzes in the Manner of Isadora Duncan (Page 90)
Music Johannes Brahms; *Choreography* Frederick Ashton; *Lighting* Mark Jonathan. **WP:** 15 June 1976, Ballet Rambert gala; **CP:** 5 April 2000, Bham (Rep). **Perf.** 2000: Bham (Rep), Brad, Plym, Sland; 2004: Bham, Barnstaple, New York, Truro, Yeovil

Five Tangos (Pages 124 & 125)
Music Astor Piazzolla; *Choreography* Hans van Manen; *Designs* Jean-Paul Vroom; *Lighting* John Hall. **WP:** 3 November 1977, Dutch National Ballet; **CP:** 31 October 1991, Bham. **Perf.** 1991: Bham, Leeds; 1992: Lon; 1999: Bham; 2004: Barnstaple, Truro, Yeovil; 2005: Durham, Hull, Mbrough, York

Flowers of the Forest
Music Malcolm Arnold *and* Benjamin Britten; *Choreography* David Bintley; *Designs* Jan Blake; *Lighting* John B. Read. **WP:** 14 June 1985, SWRB; **CP:** 19 Oct 1992, Bham. **Perf.** 1992: Bham, Cardiff, Plym; 1993: Oxford

Four Seasons, The (Pages 130 & 131)
Music Antonio Vivaldi; *Choreography* Oliver Hindle; *Designs* Conor Murphy; *Lighting* Charles Balfour. **WP:** 9 March 2005, BRB, Bham. **Perf.** 2005: Bham, Plym; 2007: Bham, Salfd

Four Seasons, The: Summer and Autumn (Pages 130 & 131)
Music Antonio Vivaldi; *Choreography* Oliver Hindle; *Designs* Conor Murphy; *Lighting* Charles Balfour. **WP:** 9 March 2005, BRB, Bham. **Perf.** 2006: Exeter, Poole, Truro; 2007: Durham, Mbrough, York

Four Temperaments
Music Paul Hindemith; *Choreography* George Balanchine © The George Balanchine Trust; *Rehearsed by* Victoria Simon. **WP:** 20 November 1946, Ballet Society; **CP:** 16 October 1997, Bham. **Perf.** 1997: Bham, Brad, Bristol, Sland

Galanteries (Page 156)
Music Wolfgang Amadeus Mozart; *Choreography* David Bintley; *Designs* Jan Blake; *Lighting* John B. Read. **WP:** 12 July 1986, The Royal Ballet; **CP:** 6 March 1992, Bham. **Perf.** 1992: Bham, Lon; 1994: Bham, Brad, Bristol, Edin, Plym; 2009: Bham, Durham, King's Lynn, Sheff, York

Giselle
Music Adolph Adam and others; *Choreography* Marius Petipa *after* Jean Coralli *and* Jules Perrot; *Additional choreography* Frederick Ashton; *Revised by* Nicolai Sergeyev (from 1992); *Scenario* Théophile Gaultier; *After a theme of* Heinrich Heine; *Production* Peter Wright; *Designs* Peter Farmer; *Lighting* John B. Read. **WP:** 28 June 1841, Paris Opéra Ballet; **CP:** 3 March 1992, Bham. **Perf.** 1992: Bham, Brad, Canterbury, Ebourne, Lon

Giselle (Pages 34-37)
Music Adolph Adam; *Revised by* Joseph Horowitz; *Choreography* Marius Petipa *after* Jean Coralli *and* Jules Perrot *with additional choreography by* David Bintley; *Scenario* Théophile Gautier *and* Jules Henri Vernoy de Saint-Georges; *Production* Galina Samsova *and* David Bintley *assisted by* Desmond Kelly; *Designs* Hayden Griffin; *Lighting* Mark Jonathan. **WP:** 28 June 1841, Paris Opéra Ballet; **CP:** 30 Sept 1999, Bham. **Perf.** 1999: Bham, Brad, Plym, Sland; 2000: Lon (ROH), Salfd; 2003: Bham, Plym, Sland; 2008: Bham

Green Table, The
Music Fritz A. Cohen; *Book and choreography* Kurt Jooss; *Designs* Hein Heckroth; *Staged by* Anna Markard; *Lighting and masks* Herman Markard. **WP:** 3 July 1932, Folkwang Tanzbühne; **CP:** 19 October 1992, Bham. **Perf.** 1992: Bham, Cardiff, Plym; 1993: Lon, Oxford, Shton; 1994: Bham

Grosse Fuge (Page 126)
Music Ludwig van Beethoven; *Choreography and costumes* Hans van Manen; *Sets* Jean-Paul Vroom; *Lighting* Jan Hofstra. **WP:** 8 April 1971, Netherlands Dance Theatre; **CP:** 25 February 1998, Bham. **Perf.** 1998: Bham, Brad, Bristol, Lpool, Man, Plym; 2010: Bham, Durham, King's Lynn, Sheff, York

Hermanas, Las
Music Frank Martin; *Choreography* Kenneth MacMillan; *Designs* Nicholas Georgiadis. **WP:** 13 July 1963, Stuttgart Ballet; **CP:** 27 June 1995, Bham. **Perf.** 1995: Bham

Hobson's Choice (Pages 182-186)
Music Paul Reade; *Choreography* David Bintley; *Designs* Hayden Griffin (Costumes co-designed with Claudia Mayer); *Lighting* John B. Read. **WP:** 13 February 1989, SWRB; **CP:** 9 April 1991, Cardiff. **Perf.** 1991: Bham, Brad, Bristol, Cardiff, Lon, Lon (ROH), Plym; 1993: Bham, Lon, Shton; 1995: Bham, Bristol, Plym; 1999: Bham, Lpool; 2002: Bham, Plym, Salfd; 2005: Bham, Edin, Lon, Plym, Sland

In the Upper Room (Page 122)
Music Philip Glass; *Choreography* Twyla Tharp © 1992; *Costumes* Norma Kamali; *Lighting* Jennifer Tipton. **WP:** 28 August 1986, Twyla Tharp Dance; **CP:** 10 February 1999, Lon. **Perf.** 1999: Bham, Lpool, Lon, Plym, Sland; 2001: Bham (Alex), Plym, Sland; 2005: Bham, Plym; 2010: Bham, Lon, Plym

Into the Ferment (Page 147)
Music James MacMillan; *Choreography* Jonathan Payn; *Designs* Mark Simmonds; *Lighting* Peter Teigen. **WP:** 15 June 2005, BRB, Bham. **Perf.** 2005: Bham

Inscape
Music Peter McGowan; *Choreography* Graham Lustig; *Designs* Henk Schut; *Lighting* Graham Large. **WP:** 6 August 1991, Lon (ROH); **CP:** 6 August 1991, Lon (ROH). **Perf.** 1991: Lon (ROH)

Jazz Calendar (Pages 82 & 83)
Music Richard Rodney Bennett; *Choreography* Frederick Ashton; *Designs* Derek Jarman; *Lighting* John Hall. **WP:** 9 January 1968, The Royal Ballet; **CP:** 30 October 1990, Bham. **Perf.** 1990: Bham; 1991: Lon (ROH)

Job (Pages 65 & 66)
Music Ralph Vaughan Williams; *Choreography* Ninette de Valois; *Revival* Joy Newton *assisted by* Jean Bedells; *Designs* John Piper; *Lighting* Michael Benthall. **WP:** 5 July 1931, Carmago Society; **CP:** 11 June 1993, Bham. **Perf.** 1993: Bham, Cov, Lon (ROH); 1994: Bham

Krishna
Music Hariprasad Chaurasia; *Choreography* Nahid Siddiqui; *Designs* Kate Ford; *Lighting* Peter Teigen. **WP:** 24 September 2003, BRB, Bham. **Perf.** 2003: Bham, Plym, Sland

Lady and the Fool, The (Page 94)
Music Giuseppe Verdi; *Arranged by* Charles Mackerras; *Scenario and Choreography* John Cranko; *Designs* Kate Ford; *Lighting* Tim Mitchell. **WP:** 25 February 1954, SWTB; **CP:** 5 October 2005, Bham. **Perf.** 2005: Bham, Edin, Lon, Plym, Sland; 2010: Bham

Libramenta (Page 145)
Music Béla Bartók; *Choreography* Oliver Hindle; *Designs* Lakis Yenethli; *Lighting* Aaron McPeake. **WP:** 10 March 1995, BRB, Bham. **Perf.** 1995: Bham

License My Roving Hands
Music Jimi Hendrix; *Choreography* William Tuckett; *Designs* Candida Cook; *Lighting* John B. Read. **WP:** 15 May 1991, BRB, Lon. **Perf.** 1991: Bham, Lon, Shton

Monotones II
Music Erik Satie; *Choreography and designs* Frederick Ashton; *Lighting* Nicholas Ware. **WP:** 24 March 1965, Royal Ballet Benevolent Fund Gala; **CP:** 7 February 2004, Bham (SH). **Perf.** 2004: Barnstaple, Bham (SH), Truro, Yeovil; 2005: Durham, Hull, Mbrough, York

Mozartiana (Page 115)
Music Pyotr Ilyich Tchaikovsky; *Choreography* George Balanchine © The George Balanchine Trust; *Costumes* Rouben Ter-Artunian; *Staged by* Maria Calegari. **WP:** 4 June 1981, New York City Ballet; **CP:** 2 May 1996, Bham. **Perf.** 1996: Bham; 2009: Bham, Chelt, Exeter, Poole, Truro

Nine Sinatra Songs (Page 121)
Songs sung by Frank Sinatra; *Choreography* Twyla Tharp © 1992; *Scenic design originally by* Santo Loquasto; *Original costume design by* Oscar de la Renta; *Lighting originally by* Jennifer Tipton. **WP:** 14 October 1982, Twyla Tharp Dance; **CP:** 23 June 2006, Poole. **Perf.** 2006: Exeter, Poole, Truro; 2007: Bham, Durham, Lon, Mbrough, Plym, Salfd, Sland, York

Nutcracker, The (Pages 41-48)
Music Pyotr Ilyich Tchaikovsky; *Choreography* Peter Wright, Lev Ivanov *and* Vincent Redmon; *Production* Peter Wright; *Designs* John F. Macfarlane, *Lighting* David A. Finn. **WP:** 18 December 1892, Mariinsky Ballet; **CP:** 29 December 1990, Bham. **Perf.** 1990: Bham; 1991: Bham; 1992: Bham; 1993: Bham; 1994: Bham, Lon (Col); 1995: Bham; 1996: Bham; 1997: Bham; 1998: Bham, Lon (Lyc); 1999: Bham; 2000: Salfd; 2001: Bham; 2002: Bham; 2004: Bham; 2006: Bham; 2007: Bham; 2008: Bham; 2009: Bham

Nutcracker Sweeties, The (Pages 206 & 207)
Music Duke Ellington *and* Billy Strayhorn; *Choreography* David Bintley; *Costumes* Jasper Conran; *Sets* Peter J. Davison, *Lighting* Peter Mumford. **WP:** 26 September 1996, BRB, Bham. **Perf.** 1996: Bham, Brad, Bristol, Plym, Sland; 1997: Bham, Lon (ROH), Man, Plym, Shton; 1999: Bham, Brad, Plym, Sland; 2000: Chicago, Lon (ROH), New York (CC), Salfd; 2004: Bham, Lon, Plym

Orpheus
Music Igor Stravinsky; *Choreography* George Balanchine © The George Balanchine Trust; *Staged by* Karin von Aroldingen, Nilas Martins *and* Victoria Simon; *Designs* Isamu Noguchi; *Lighting* Perry Silvey. **WP:** 28 April 1948, Ballet Society; **CP:** 16 October 1997, Bham. **Perf.** 1997: Bham, Brad, Bristol, Sland

Orpheus Suite, The (Pages 197-199)
Music Colin Towns; *Choreography* David Bintley; *Sets and lighting* Steven Scott; *Costumes* Kandis Cook. **WP:** 6 October 2004, BRB, Bham. **Perf.** 2004: Bham, Lon, Plym; 2008: Bham, Oxford, Plym, Sland

Paramour (Page 144)
Music Francis Poulenc; *Choreography* Graham Lustig; *Designs* Nadine Baylis; *Lighting* John B. Read. **WP:** 19 March 1987, SWRB; **CP:** 2 February 1993, Lon. **Perf.** 1993: Lon

Patineurs, Les
Music Giacomo Meyerbeer; *Arranged by* Constant Lambert; *Choreography* Frederick Ashton; *Designs* William Chappell; *Lighting* John B. Read. **WP:** 16 February 1937, Vic-Wells Ballet; **CP:** 26 September 1996, Bham. **Perf.** 1996: Bham, Brad, Bristol, Plym, Sland

Paquita (Pages 26 & 27)
Music Ludwig Minkus; *Orchestrated by* Barry Wordsworth; *Choreography* Marius Petipa; *Production* Galina Samsova; *Designs* Peter Farmer; *Lighting* John Hall. **WP:** 27 December 1881, Bolshoi Ballet; **CP:** 15 May 1991, Lon. **Perf.** 1991: Bham, Lon, Lon (ROH), Shton; 1994: Bham; 2007: Bham, Lon, Plym, Sland

Petits Riens, Les (Page 208)
Music Wolfgang Amadeus Mozart; *Choreography* David Bintley; *Costumes* Claire Leadbeater; *Lighting* Nicholas Ware. **WP:** 20 July 1991, Royal Ballet School; **CP:** 19 April 2005, Bath. **Perf.** 2005: Bath, Bham, Exeter, Truro, Yeovil

Petrushka (Page 51)
Music Igor Stravinsky; *Choreography* Mikhail Fokine; *Designs* Alexandre Benois; *Producer* John Auld; *Lighting* John B. Read (Peter Teigen from 2008). **WP:** 13 June 1911, Ballets Russes; **CP:** 25 October 1991, Bham. **Perf.** 1991: Bham, Leeds, Lon, Plym; 2008: Bham, Cardiff (WMC), Edin, Lon

Pillar of Fire (Page 120)
Music Arnold Schönberg; *Choreography* Anthony Tudor; *Staged by* Sallie Wilson; *Designs* Joe Mielziner; *Lighting* John Hall. **WP:** 8 April 1942, American Ballet Theatre; **CP:** 10 March 1995, Bham. **Perf.** 1995: Bham, Brad, Lon (ROH), Ludwigshafen, Shton, Stuttgart

Pineapple Poll (Pages 92 & 93)
Music Arthur Sullivan; *Arranged by* Charles Mackerras; *Choreography* John Cranko; *Designs* Osbert Lancaster; *Lighting* Neil Austin. **WP:** 13 March 1951, SWTB; **CP:** 7 February 1995, Lon. **Perf.** 1995: Lon; 2006: Durham, Grimsby, Sheff, York; 2007: Bham, Chelt, Poole, Salfd, Truro

Powder (Pages 134 & 135)
Music Wolfgang Amadeus Mozart; *Choreography* Stanton Welch; *Designs* Kandis Cook; *Lighting* Mark Jonathan. **WP:** 7 October 1998, Bham. **Perf.** 1998: Bham, Brad, Bristol, Plym, Sland; 2001: Bham (Alex), Plym, Sland; 2002: Bham, Edin; 2009: Bham, Lon, Plym, Sland

Prodigal Son (Page 62)
Music Sergei Prokofiev; *Choreography* George Balanchine © The George Balanchine Trust; *Staged by* Patricia Neary; *Designs* Georges Rouault; *Lighting* Peter Teigen after the original designs. **WP:** 21 May 1929, Ballets Russes; **CP:** 21 June 1994, Bham. **Perf.** 1994: Bham, Bristol, Man, Plym; 1995: Lon; 2001: Brad, Plym, Sland; 2005: Bham, Plym

Prospect Before Us, The (Pages 67 & 68)
Music William Boyce; *Arranged by* Constant Lambert; *Choreography* Ninette de Valois; *Staging* Jean Bedells *with assistance from* David Bintley *and* Marion Tait; *Designs* Roger Furse *after* Thomas Rowlandson; *Lighting* Mark Jonathan. **WP:** 4 July 1940, SWB; **CP:** 3 June 1998, Bham. **Perf.** 1998: Bham; 1999: Lon

Protecting Veil, The (Pages 187-189)
Music John Taverner; *Choreography* David Bintley; *Designs* Ruari Murchison; *Lighting* Mark Jonathan. **WP:** 3 June 1998, BRB, Bham. **Perf.** 1998: Bham, Bristol, Brad, Plym, Sland; 1999: Lon

Pulcinella (Page 129)
Music Igor Stravinsky; *Choreography* Kim Brandstrup; *Sets and lighting* Steven Scott; *Costumes* Kandis Cook. **WP:** 3 May 2006, Bham. **Perf.** 2006: Bham, Lon, Plym, Sland

Raymonda Act III (Page 40)
Music Alexander Glazunov; *Choreography and production* Rudolf Nureyev; *Designs* Barry Kay; *Lighting* Peter Teigen. **WP:** 18 January 1898, Mariinsky Ballet; **CP:** 9 October 2008, Bham. **Perf.** 2008: Bham

Rendezvous, Les
Music Daniel Auber; *Arranged and orchestrated by* Constant Lambert; *Choreography* Frederick Ashton; *Designs* William Chappell. **WP:** 5 December 1933, Vic-Wells Ballet; **CP:** 15 May 1991, Lon. **Perf.** 1991: Lon

Rite of Spring, The (Pages 54 & 55)
Music Igor Stravinsky; *Choreography* Vaslav Nijinsky; *Reconstructed and staged by* Millicent Hodson; *Designs* Nicholas Roerich; *Reconstructed and supervised by* Kenneth Archer; *Lighting* Peter Teigen. **WP:** 22 May 1913, Ballets Russes; **CP:** 8 June 2005, Bham. **Perf.** 2005: Bham

Romeo and Juliet (Pages 100-106)
Music Sergei Prokofiev; *Choreography* Kenneth MacMillan; *Designs* Paul Andrews; *Lighting* Hans-Åke Sjöquist (John B. Read from 1998). **WP:** 9 February 1965, The Royal Ballet; **CP:** 1 June 1992, Bham. **Perf.** 1992: Bham, Bristol, Man (OH), Oxford, Shton; 1993: Hong Kong, Lon (ROH); 1994: Bham, Edin; 1998: Bham, Brad, Bristol, Plym, Sland; 2002: Bham, Brad, Plym, Sland; 2005: Bham, Brad, Plym, Salfd, Sland; 2006: Bham, Lon, Plym, Sland; 2009: Beijing, Guangzhou, Shanghai; 2010: Bham, Cardiff (WMC), Lon, Plym, Salfd, Sland

Sacred Symphony
Music Andrzej Panufnik; *Choreography* Oliver Hindle; *Designs* Jan Blake; *Lighting* Graham Large. **WP:** 10 May 1991, BRB, Lon. **Perf.** 1991: Bham, Lon, Shton

Sanctum (Pages 138 & 139)
Music Maurice Ravel *and* Christopher Rouse; *Choreography* Lila York; *Designs* Theoni V. Aldredge; *Lighting* John B. Read. **WP:** 16 May 1997, BRB, Shton. **Perf.** 1997: Bham, Lon (ROH), Man, Plym, Shton; 2002: Bham

Scènes de ballet (Page 78)
Music Igor Stravinsky; *Choreography* Frederick Ashton; *Staged by* Malin Thoors-Watt; *Designs* André Beaurepaire; *Lighting* Mark Jonathan. **WP:** 11 February 1948, The Royal Ballet; **CP:** 14 April 2000, Bham (Rep). **Perf.** 2000: Bham (Rep), Brad, Plym, Sland; 2005: Bham, Hamburg

Seasons, The (Pages 190 & 191)
Music Giuseppe Verdi; *Choreography* David Bintley; *Designs* Jean-Marc Puissant; *Lighting* Mark Jonathan. **WP:** 13 September 2001, BRB, Lon. **Perf.** 2001: Bham, Brad, Lon, Plym, Sland; 2006: Bham, Plym

Serenade (Pages 110 & 111)
Music Pyotr Ilyich Tchaikovsky; *Choreography* George Balanchine © The George Balanchine Trust; *Staged by* Patricia Neary; *Costumes* Karinska; *Lighting* Ronald Bates (Peter Teigen from 2009). **WP:** 1 March 1935, American Ballet Theatre; **CP:** 22 February 1994, Bham. **Perf.** 1994: Bham, Brad, Ebourne, Lpool, Lon (ROH), Nhton, Sland; 1995: Bham, Shton; 1997: Bham, Brad, Bristol, Sland; 2009: Bham, Lon (Col), Plym, Salfd, Sland

Shakespeare Suite, The (Pages 179-181)
Music Duke Ellington *and* Billy Strayhorn; *Choreography* David Bintley; *Sets and lighting* Steven Scott; *Costumes* Jasper Conran. **WP:** 6 October 1999, BRB, Bham. **Perf.** 1999: Bham, Brad, Plym, Sland; 2000: Chicago, Lon (ROH), New York (CC), Salfd; 2004: Bham, Lon, Plym; 2008: Bham, Oxford, Plym, Sland

Slaughter on Tenth Avenue (Page 114)
Music Richard Rodgers; *Choreography* George Balanchine © The George Balanchine Trust; *Staged by* Susan Hendl; *Designs* Kate Ford; *Lighting* Nicholas Royle (Johnny Westall-Eyre from 2010). **WP:** 11 April 1936, as part of *On Your Toes!*; **CP:** 6 October 1999, Bham. **Perf.** 1999: Bham, Brad, Plym, Sland; 2000: Chicago, Lon (ROH), New York (CC), Salfd; 2010: Bham, Chelt, Lon, Plym, Poole, Truro

Sleeping Beauty, The (Pages 28-33)
Music Pyotr Ilyich Tchaikovsky; *Choreography* Marius Petipa *and* Peter Wright; *Production* Peter Wright; *Designs* Philip Prowse; *Lighting* John B. Read (Mark Jonathan from 2003). **WP:** 16 January 1890, Mariinsky Ballet; **CP:** 2 November 1990, Bham. **Perf.** 1990: Bham, Edin, Glasgow; 1993: Bangkok, Bham, Brad, Lon (ROH), Norwich, Plym; 1995: Bham, Plym; 1997: Bham, Brad, Lpool, Plym, Sland; 2003: Bham (NIA), Plym, Salfd; 2006: Bham, Oxford, Plym, Salfd, Sland; 2007: Virginia; 2010: Bham, Lon (Col), Plym, Salfd, Sland

Small Worlds (Page 143)
Music Igor Stravinsky; *Choreography* Kit Holder; *Designs* Helen Fownes-Davies; *Lighting* Peter Teigen. **WP:** 2 June 2006, BRB, Bham. **Perf.** 2006: Bham; 2007: Durham, Mbrough, York; 2008: Chelt, Exeter, Poole, Truro

Snow Queen, The (Pages 176 & 177)
Music Bramwell Tovey *after* Modest Mussorgsky; *Choreography* David Bintley; *Designs* Terry Bartlett; *Lighting* John B. Read. **WP:** 28 April 1986, SWRB; **CP:** 22 October 1992, Bham. **Perf.** 1992: Bham, Plym; 1993: Bham, Cardiff, Lon, Oxford

Solitaire (Page 95)
Music Malcolm Arnold; *Choreography* Kenneth MacMillan; *Designs* Kim Beresford; *Lighting* Peter Teigen. **WP:** 7 June 1956, SWTB; **CP:** 5 October 2005, Bham. **Perf.** 2005: Bham, Edin, Lon, Plym, Sland; 2006: Durham, Grimsby, Sheff, York; 2007: Chelt, Poole, Truro

Song of the Earth
Music Gustav Mahler; *Choreography* Kenneth MacMillan; *Staging* Monica Parker; *Designs* Nicholas Georgiadis; *Lighting* John B. Read. **WP:** 7 November 1965, Stuttgart Ballet; **CP:** 25 February 1997, Bham. **Perf.** 1997: Bham, Brad, Plym, Sland

Sons of Horus, The (Page 196)
Music Peter McGowan; *Choreography* David Bintley; *Designs* Terry Bartlett; *Lighting* Peter Teigen after the original design. **WP:** 30 October 1985, The Royal Ballet; **CP:** 24 September 2003, Bham. **Perf.** 2003: Bham, Plym, Sland

Stravinsky Violin Concerto
Music Igor Stravinsky; *Choreography* George Balanchine © The George Balanchine Trust; *Staged by* Karin von Aroldingen *and* Richard Tanner; *Lighting* Peter Teigen. **WP:** 18 June 1972, New York City Ballet; **CP:** 14 February 2007, Bham. **Perf.** 2007: Bham, Plym, Salfd, Sland

Street (Page 146)
Music William Russo; *Choreography* Matthew Hart; *Designs* Peter Farmer; *Lighting* John Hall. **WP:** 1 June 1993, BRB, Bham. **Perf.** 1993: Bham, Plym; 1995: Lon

'Still Life' at the Penguin Café (Pages 170-173)
Music Simon Jeffes; *Choreography* David Bintley; *Designs* Hayden Griffin; *Lighting* John B. Read. **WP:** 9 March 1988, The Royal Ballet; **CP:** 8 May 1996, Bham. **Perf.** 1996: Bham, Brad, Lon (ROH); 1998: Bham, Brad, Bristol, Plym, Sland; 1999: Bham, Lpool; 2001: Bham, Brad, Lon, Plym, Sland; 2009: Bham, Lon (Col), Plym, Salfd, Sland

Sum of the Parts, The
Music Timothy Sutton; *Choreography* Jennifer Jackson; *Designs* Henk Schut. **WP:** 29 January 1993, BRB, Stafford. **Perf.** 1993: Hereford, Stafford, Telford

Swan Lake (Pages 19-25)
Music Pyotr Ilyich Tchaikovsky; *Choreography* Marius Petipa, Lev Ivanov *and* Peter Wright; *Production* Peter Wright *and* Galina Samsova; *Designs* Philip Prowse, *Lighting* John B. Read (Peter Teigen from 2001). **WP:** 27 January 1895, Mariinsky Ballet; **CP:** 18 February 1991, Plym. **Perf.** 1991: Bham, Lpool, Lon (ROH), Man, Plym, Shton, Sland; 1992: Bham, Oxford; 1994: Bham, Bristol, Ebourne, Man, Plym, Shton; 1995: Bham, Frankfurt, Fukushima, Hiroshima, Kofu, Kumamoto, Kurashiki, Lpool, Matsuyama, Nagoya, Numazu, Osaka, Sland, Tokyo, Utsunomiya, Yokohama; 1996: Bham, Brad, Bristol, Plym, Sland; 2001: Bham (NIA), Brad, Lon, Plym, Sland; 2002: Salfd; 2004: Bham; 2008: Belfast, Bham, Oxford, Plym, Salfd, Sland; 2010: Bham, Virginia

Sylphides, Les
Music Frederick Chopin; *Orchestrated by* Roy Douglas (from 1992); *Choreography* Mikhail Fokine; *Producer* Galina Samsova; *Designs* Alexandre Benois (Peter Farmer from 1992); *Lighting* John Hall. **WP:** December 1906, Mariinsky Ballet; **CP:** 31 October 1991, Bham. **Perf.** 1991: Bham, Leeds, Plym; 1992: Bham, Brad, Canterbury, Ebourne, Lon; 1993: Cardiff, Oxford

Sylvia (Pages 209-213)
Music Léo Delibes; *Choreography* David Bintley; *Designs* Sue Blane; *Lighting* David Hersey (Peter Teigen, revised production 2009). **WP:** 14 June 1876, Palais Garnier, Paris; **CP:** 26 October 1993, Bham; Revised production: 25 February 2009, Bham. **Perf.** 1993: Bham, Plym; 1994: Bham, Lon (ROH), Lpool, Nhton, Shton; 2009: Bham, Lon (Col), Plym, Salfd, Sland

Symphonic Variations
Music César Franck; *Choreography* Frederick Ashton; *Production* Michael Somes; *Designs* Sophie Fedorovitch; *Lighting* John B. Read. **WP:** 24 April 1946, SWB; **CP:** 19 October 1992, Bham. **Perf.** 1992: Bham, Plym; 1998: Bham

Symphony in Three Movements (Page 113)
Music Igor Stravinsky; *Choreography* George Balanchine © The George Balanchine Trust; *Staged by* Patricia Neary; *Lighting* John Hall (Peter Teigen from 2007). **WP:** 18 June 1972, New York City Ballet; **CP:** 9 November 1990, Bham. **Perf.** 1990: Bham; 1991: Lon (ROH), Plym; 1994: Bham, Bristol, Man, Plym; 1998: Bham, Brad, Bristol, Lpool, Man, Plym; 2007: Bham, Plym, Salfd, Sland

Take Five (Page 214)
Music The Dave Brubeck Quartet; *Transcribed by* Colin Towns; *Choreography* David Bintley; *Designs* Jean-Marc Puissant; *Lighting* Peter Mumford. **WP:** 22 June 2007, BRB, Truro. **Perf.** 2007: Chelt, Poole, Truro; 2008: Bham, Durham, King's Lynn, Oxford, Plym, Sland, York

Tarantella
Music Louis Gottschalk; *Arranged by* Hershy Kay; *Choreography* George Balanchine © The George Balanchine Trust. **WP:** 7 January 1964, New York City Ballet; **CP:** 11 March 2004, Bham. **Perf.** 2004: Bham

Theme and Variations (Page 116)
Music Pyotr Ilyich Tchaikovsky; *Choreography* George Balanchine © The George Balanchine Trust; *Staged by* Patricia Neary; *Designs* Peter Farmer; *Lighting* John B. Read. **WP:** 26 November 1947, American Ballet Theatre; **CP:** 30 October 1990, Bham. **Perf.** 1990: Bham; 1991: Cardiff, Lon (ROH), Sland; 1994: Bham, Plym; 1995: Bham, Brad, Lon (ROH); 1996: Bham, Brad, Lon (ROH); 2010: Bham

Tombeaux (Pages 174 & 175)
Music William Walton; *Choreography* David Bintley; *Staged by* Grant Coyle; *Designs* Jasper Conran; *Lighting* John B. Read. **WP:** 11 February 1993, The Royal Ballet; **CP:** 16 May 1997, Shton. **Perf.** 1997: Bham, Man, Plym, Shton; 2002: Bham

Tricorne, Le (Pages 56 & 57)
Music Manuel de Falla; *Choreography* Léonide Massine *Staged by* Lorca Massine; *Designs* Pablo Picasso; *Lighting* John Hall. **WP:** 22 July 1919, Ballets Russes; **CP:** 11 October 1994, Bham. **Perf.** 1994: Bham, Brad, Bristol, Edin, Plym; 1995: Lon (ROH), Shton

Tweedledum and Tweedledee
Music Percy Grainger; *Choreography* Frederick Ashton; *Lighting* Mark Jonathan. **WP:** 28 November 1977, Gala in Aid of the Friends of One-parent Families; **CP:** 5 April 2000, Bham (Rep). **Perf.** 2000: Bham (Rep), Brad, Plym, Sland; 2001: Bham (SH), Ross on Wye; 2004: Barnstaple, Truro, Yeovil

Twilight (Page 123)
Music John Cage; *Choreography* Hans van Manen; *Designs* Jean-Paul Vroom; *Lighting* Jan Hofstra. **WP:** 20 June 1972, Dutch National Ballet; **CP:** 2 February 1993, Lon. **Perf.** 1993: Brad, Lon, Shton; 2008: Durham, King's Lynn, York; 2009: Chelt, Exeter, Poole, Truro

Two Pigeons, The (Pages 70 & 71)
Music André Messager; *Adapted and arranged by* John Lanchbery; *Choreography* Frederick Ashton; *Designs* Jacques Dupont; *Lighting* Mark Jonathan. **WP:** 14 February 1961, RBTC; **CP:** 5 April 2000, Bham (Rep). **Perf.** 2000: Bham (Rep), Brad, Plym, Sland; 2004: Bham, Lon, New York, Plym; 2009: Bham

Valses nobles et sentimentales
Music Maurice Ravel; *Choreography* Frederick Ashton; *Designs* Sophie Fedorovitch; *Lighting* John B. Read. **WP:** 1 October 1947, SWTB; **CP:** 10 May 1991, Lon. **Perf.** 1991: Lon

Voices of Spring
Music Johann Strauss II; *Choreography* Frederick Ashton; *Staged by* Lynn Seymour; *Lighting* Mark Jonathan. **WP:** 31 December 1977, as part of Royal Opera's *Die Fledermaus*; **CP:** 5 April 2000, Bham (Rep). **Perf.** 2000: Bham (Rep), Brad, Plym, Sland; 2008: Bham (SH)

Walk to the Paradise Garden
Music Frederick Delius; *Choreography* Frederick Ashton; *Designs* William Chappell; *Lighting* Mark Jonathan. **WP:** 5 November 1972, The Royal Ballet; **CP:** 5 April 2000, Bham (Rep). **Perf.** 2000: Bham (Rep), Brad, Plym, Sland

Western Symphony
Music Traditional American melodies arranged by Hershey Kay; *Choreography* George Balanchine © The George Balanchine Trust; *Staged by* Patricia Neary; *Sets* John Boyt; *Costumes* Karinska; *Lighting* Perry Silvey. **WP:** 7 September 1954, New York City Ballet; **CP:** 2 October 2002, Bham. **Perf.** 2002: Bham, Plym, Sland; 2003: Brad, Edin, Salfd; 2004: Bham, Lon, Plym

DIVERTISSEMENTS
Unless otherwise listed, please see main repertory for details.

Aladdin: Act II pas de deux
Music Carl Davis; *Choreography* David Bintley; *Costumes* Sue Blane. **WP:** 15 November 2008, National Ballet of Japan; **CP:** 20 February 2010, Bham (SH). **Perf.** 2010: Bham, Bham (SH)

Apollo: solo variation and pas de deux
Perf. 2006: Bham (SH); 2008: Bham

Beauty and the Beast: Act I pas de deux
Perf. 2010: Bham

Birthday Offering: Waltz pas de deux
Perf. 1996: Bham (SH)

Boutique fantasque: Can-can *Music* Gioacchino Rossini; *Arranged by* Ottorino Respighi; *Choreography* Leonide Massine; *Costumes* Andre Derain. **WP:** 5 June 1919, Ballets Russes; **CP:** 31 January 1992, Bham (SH). **Perf.** 1992: Bham (SH), Lon (Bar)

Card Game: Third Deal
Perf. 2008: Bham (SH)

Carmina burana: Second Seminarian's solo and Tanz
Perf. 2010: Bham

Checkmate: Black Queen's solo
CP: 29 January 1993, Stafford. **Perf.** 1993: Hereford, Stafford, Telford; 2005: Bham (SH)

Concerto: pas de deux
CP: 31 January 1992, Bham (SH). **Perf.** 1992: Bham (SH), Lon (Bar); 1993: Hereford, Stafford, Telford; 1997: Bham (SH); 2005: Bham (SH); 2008: Bham (SH)

Concerto barocco: Third movement
Perf. 2004: Bham

Coppélia: Magic scene
Perf. 1996: Bham (SH); 2007: Bham (SH)

Coppélia: Dawn and Prayer solos
Perf. 2006: Bham (SH)

Coppélia: Act III pas de deux
Perf. 2003: Bham (SH)

Corsaire, Le: pas de deux *Music* Riccardo Drigo; *Choreography* Joseph Mazilier *after* Marius Petipa. **WP:** 23 January 1856, Paris; **CP:** 31 October 1991, Bham. **Perf.** 1991: Bham; 2001: Bham (SH); 2010: Bham (SH)

Dance House, The: pas de deux
Perf. 2001: Bham; 2006: Bham (SH)

Diana and Actaeon pas de deux *Music* Riccardo Drigo; *Choreography* Agrippina Vaganova. **WP:** 1932, Kirov Ballet, as part of *La Esmerelda*; **CP:** 30 March 2007, Bham (SH). **Perf.** 2007: Bham (SH)

Don Quixote: pas de deux *Music* Ludwig Minkus; *Orchestrated by* Robert Irving (from 1993); *Choreography* Marius Petipa; *Designs* André Levasseur. **WP:** 26 December 1869, Bolshoi Ballet; **CP:** 31 January 1992, Bham (SH). **Perf.** 1992: Bham (SH), Lon (Bar); 1993: Brad, Lon, Shton; 1996: Bham (SH); 2000: Bham (SH), Man (BW), Preston; 2005: Bham (SH)

Dream, The: pas de deux
Perf. 1993: Bham (SH); 1994: Bham (SH); 1997: Bham (SH); 2003: Bham (SH)

Elite Syncopations: Bethena Concert Waltz
Perf. 1993: Bham (SH); 1998: Bham (SH)

Elite Syncopations: Excerpts
Perf. 1993: Hereford, Stafford, Telford

Elite Syncopations: Friday Night
Perf. 2004: Bham (SH)

Enigma Variations: Nimrod
Perf. 2008: Bham

Façade: Tango
Perf. 1993: Hereford, Stafford, Telford; 1997: Bham (SH); 2002: Bham (SH); 2004: Bham

Façade: Polka
Perf. 2002: Bham (SH)

Façade: Popular Song
Perf. 1994: Bham (SH)

Far from the Madding Crowd: Sword pas de deux
Perf. 1998: Bham (SH); 2001: Bham

Fille mal gardée, La: Clog Dance
Perf. 1993: Bham (SH); 1994: Bham (SH); 1996: Bham (SH); 2004: Bham

Fille mal gardée, La: Fanny Elssler pas de deux
Perf. 2000: Bham (SH), Man (BW), Preston; 2004: Bham (SH)

Flower Festival in Genzano: pas de deux *Music* Edvard Helstedt; *Choreography* August Bournonville; *Costumes* Richard Beer. **WP:** 19 December 1858, The Royal Danish Ballet; **CP:** 31 January 1992, Bham (SH). **Perf.** 1992: Bham (SH), Lon (Bar)

Flowers of the Forest: Four Scottish Dances
Perf. 1993: Hereford, Stafford, Telford; 2001: Bham, Bham (SH); Ross on Wye; 2010: Bham (SH)

Flowers of the Forest: pas de deux
Perf. 1993: Bham (SH)

Giselle: Harvest pas de deux (Wright production)
Perf. 1994: Bham (SH)

Giselle: Act II pas de deux (Bintley/Samsova production)
Perf. 2008: Bham (SH)

Giselle: Harvest pas de deux (Bintley/Samsova production)
Perf. 2000: Bham (SH), Man (BW), Preston

Hobson's Choice: Clog Dance
Perf. 1991: Lon; 1995: Bham; 1996: Bham (SH); 1998: Bham (SH); 2005: Bham (SH); 2008: Bham

Hobson's Choice: Lily of Laguna pas de deux
Perf. 1991: Lon; 1995: Bham; 1999: Basingstoke, Bham (SH); 2001: Bham, Ross on Wye; 2005: Bham (SH)

Hobson's Choice: Will Mossop's stag night
Perf. 2010: Bham

Job: extracts
Perf. 1995: Bham

Job: Satan's solo
Perf. 2002: Bham (SH)

Lady and the Fool, The: Clown duet
Designs Richard Beer. **CP:** 24 January 2002, Bham (SH). **Perf.** 2002: Bham (SH)

Mirror Walkers, The: pas de deux
Music Pyotr Ilyich Tchaikovsky; *Choreography* Peter Wright. **WP:** 27 April 1963, Stuttgart Ballet; **CP:** 1 July 1995, Bham. **Perf.** 1995: Bham

Nutcracker, The: Grand pas de deux
Choreography Lev Ivanov. **Perf.** 1991: Cardiff, Lon; 1992: Bham (SH), Lon (Bar); 1993: Bham (SH); 1994: Bham (SH), Lpool, Sland; 1996: Bham (SH); 1998: Bham (SH); 1999: Basingstoke, Bham (SH); 2000: Bham (SH), Man (BW), Preston; 2008: Bham; 2010: Bham

Orpheus Suite, The: Opening sequence
Perf. 2010: Bham

Paquita: pas de deux
Perf. 2007: Bham (SH)

Pavane
Music Gabriel Fauré; *Choreography* Kenneth MacMillan; *Costumes* Deborah MacMillan. **WP:** 13 January 1973, The Royal Ballet; **CP:** 15 May 1991, Lon. **Perf.** 1991: Leeds, Lon; 1993: Lon

Pineapple Poll: solo and pas de trois
CP: 6 January 1991, Lon. **Perf.** 1991: Lon; 2007: Bham (SH)

Prodigal Son: pas de deux
Perf. 2008: Bham

Rake's Progress, The: Betrayed Girl
Music and libretto Gavin Gordon; *Choreography* Ninette de Valois; *Designs* Rex Whistler. **WP:** 20 May 1935, Vic-Wells Ballet; **CP:** 6 January, 1991, Lon. **Perf.** 1991: Lon

Raymonda Act III: solos and pas de trois
Perf. 2008: Bham (SH)

Romeo and Juliet: Balcony pas de deux
Perf. 1995: Bham; 1997: Bham (SH); 2002: Bham (SH); 2005: Bham (SH); 2010: Bham

Seasons, The: Spring pas de deux
WP: 30 November 2000, BRB, Blenheim. **Perf.** 2000: Blenheim; 2001: Ross on Wye; 2006: Bham (SH); 2010: Bham (SH)

Shakespeare Suite, The: Romeo and Juliet
Perf. 2007: Bham (SH)

Slaughter on Tenth Avenue: pas de deux
Perf. 2004: Bham; 2010: Bham (SH), Bham

Sleeping Beauty, The: Grand pas de deux
Perf. 1994: Bham (SH), Lpool, Sland; 1999: Basingstoke, Bham (SH); 2003: Bham (SH); 2007: Bham (SH); 2010: Bham (SH)

Sleeping Beauty, The: Rose Adagio
Perf. 2006: Bham (SH)

Sleeping Beauty, The: Bluebird pas de deux
Perf. 2002: Bham (SH); 2006: Bham (SH)

Solitaire: excerpts
Perf. 2005: Bham (SH)

Spring Waters
Music Sergei Rachmaninov; *Choreography* Asaf Messerer. **WP:** 1957, Bolshoi Ballet; **CP:** 2 February 2001, Bham (SH). **Perf.** 2001: Bham (SH); 2008: Bham, Bham (SH)

'Still Life' at the Penguin Café: Long Distance
Perf. 1999: Basingstoke, Bham (SH); 2001: Ross-on-Wye

Sylvia: Pizzicati (1993 production)
Perf. 1998: Bham (SH)

Sylvia: Pirates (1993 production)
Perf. 2001: Bham (SH)

Sylvia: Act III pas de deux (1993 production)
Perf. 2003: Bham (SH)

Sylvia: Pirates (2009 production)
Perf. 2010: Bham

Swan Lake: Black Swan pas de deux
Perf. 1992: Bham (SH), Lon (Bar); 1994: Bham (SH); 2004: Bham (SH)

Swan Lake: White Swan pas de deux
Perf. 1994: Lpool, Sland; 1997: Bham (SH); 2001: Ross-on-Wye

Swan Lake Suite
(White Swan pas de deux, Cygnets, Neapolitan Dance)
Perf. 1993: Bham (SH); 1996: Bham (SH); 2000: Bham (SH), Man (BW), Preston; 2004: Bham (SH)

Swan Lake: pas de quatre
Perf. 1993: Hereford, Stafford, Telford

Tchaikovsky pas de deux
Music Pyotr Ilyich Tchaikovsky; *Choreography* George Balanchine © The George Balanchine Trust. **WP:** 29 March 1960, New York City Ballet; **CP:** 21 August 2001, Ross on Wye. **Perf.** 2001: Ross on Wye; 2002: Bham (SH); 2003: Bham (SH); 2008: Bham (SH)

Theme and Variations: Polonaise
Perf. 1995: Bham; 2008: Bham; 2010: Bham

Tricorne, Le: Miller's Dance
Perf. 1998: Bham (SH)

Two Pigeons, The: pas de deux
CP: 30 December 1993, Bham (SH). **Perf.** 1993: Bham (SH); 1994: Bham (SH); 1998: Bham (SH); 1999: Basingstoke, Bham (SH); 2003: Bham (SH); 2010: Bham

Valse excentrique
Music Jacques Ibert; *Choreography* Kenneth MacMillan. **WP:** 10 December 1956, The Royal Ballet; **CP:** 31 January 1992, Bham (SH). **Perf.** 1992: Bham (SH), Lon (Bar); 1993: Bham (SH)

Western Symphony: Fourth movement
Perf. 2004: Bham

CHOREOGRAPHIC PROJECT BALLETS

All for a Kiss (Page 144)
Music Igor Stravinsky; *Choreography* Aonghus Hoole; *Designs* Lynsey Jackson; *Lighting* Nicholas Ware. **WP:** 2 June 2006, BRB, Bham. **Perf.** 2006: Bham

Avec Moi Ce Soir
Music Igor Stravinsky; *Choreography* Glyn Scott; *Designs* Jemima Bruntlett; *Lighting* Nicholas Ware. **WP:** 2 June 2006, BRB, Bham. **Perf.** 2006: Bham

Carnival of the Animals
Music Camille Saint-Saëns; *Choreography* David Justin ('Aviary', 'Pianists', 'Fossils' & 'The Swan'); Jonathan Payn ('Introduction and Royal March of the Lion', 'Hens and Cocks' & 'Finale'); Toby Norman-Wright ('Aquarium', 'People with Long Ears' & 'The Cuckoo in the Depths of the Woods'); Nicole Tongue ('Wild Asses', 'Tortoises', 'The Elephant' & 'Kangaroos'); *Designs* Kate Ford *and* Udi Regev; *Lighting* Nicholas Royle. **WP:** 20 February 1998, BRB, Bham. **Perf.** 1998: Bham

Concerto for Two
Music Johann Sebastian Bach; *Choreography and costumes* Laëtitia Lo Sardo; *Lighting* Steve Mackie. **WP:** 27 May 2004, BRB, Bham (Pat). **Perf.** 2004: Bham (Pat)

Dancers in the Dark
Music Joakim *and* Johann Sebastian Bach; *Choreography* Aonghus Hoole; *Costumes* Sarah Burton; *Lighting* Johnny Westall-Eyre. **WP:** 11 February 2010, BRB, Bham (Elm). **Perf.** 2010: Bham (Elm)

Danses concertantes
Music Igor Stravinsky; *Choreography* Kit Holder ('Marche Introduction' & 'Marche – Conclusion'); Aonghus Hoole ('Thème varié'); Glyn Scott ('Pas d'action'); Kosuke Yamamoto ('Pas de deux'); *Designs* Julie Bernard *and* Sharon Kilhams; *Lighting* Nicholas Ware. **WP:** 2 June 2006, BRB, Bham. **Perf.** 2006: Bham

Down and Up
Music György Ligeti *and* Arvo Pärt; *Choreography* Matthew Lawrence; *Costumes* Sarah Burton; *Lighting* Johnny Westall-Eyre. **WP:** 11 February 2010, BRB, Bham (Elm). **Perf.** 2010: Bham (Elm)

Ebony Concerto
Music Igor Stravinsky; *Choreography* Samara Downs; *Designs* Samantha Kipling; *Lighting* Nicholas Ware. **WP:** 2 June 2006, BRB, Bham. **Perf.** 2006: Bham

End of Winter, The (Page 144)
Music Igor Stravinsky; *Choreography* Kosuke Yamamoto; *Designs* Elle Harris; *Lighting* Nicholas Ware. **WP:** 2 June 2006, BRB, Bham. **Perf.** 2006: Bham

Float
Music Ryuichi Sakamoto; *Choreography* Lei Zhao; *Lighting* Steve Mackie. **WP:** 27 May 2004, BRB, Bham (Pat). **Perf.** 2004: Bham (Pat)

Follow On
Music Ludovico Einaudi; *Choreography* Nathanael Skelton; *Costumes* Sarah Burton; *Lighting* Johnny Westall-Eyre. **WP:** 11 February 2010, BRB, Bham (Elm). **Perf.** 2010: Bham (Elm)

Four Seasons, The
Music Antonio Vivaldi; *Choreography* Oliver Hindle (Summer); Shimon Kalichman (Spring: 3rd mvt); Mikaela Polley (Spring: 2nd mvt & Autumn: 1st mvt); Samira Saidi (Autumn: 3rd mvt); Asier Uriagereka (Spring: 1st mvt); Richard Whistler (Autumn: 1st mvt *pas de deux* & 2nd mvt); Yuri Zhukov (Winter); *Designs* Stephanie McIntosh *and* Christina Neeves; *Lighting* Nicholas Royle. **WP:** 20 February 1998, BRB, Bham. **Perf.** 1998: Bham; 1999: Bham, Plym, Sland

Journey, The
Music Hans Zimmer; *Choreography* Dusty Button; *Costumes* Sarah Burton; *Lighting* Johnny Westall-Eyre. **WP:** 11 February 2010, BRB, Bham (Elm). **Perf.** 2010: Bham (Elm)

Lately Undone
Music Johann Sebastian Bach; *Choreography* Kit Holder; *Costumes* Claire Leadbeater *and* Kathrin Machno; *Lighting* Steve Mackie. **WP:** 27 May 2004, BRB, Bham (Pat). **Perf.** 2004: Bham (Pat)

Moderate Becoming Good
Music Alan Taylor; *Choreography* Kit Holder; *Costumes* Sarah Burton; *Lighting* Johnny Westall-Eyre. **WP:** 11 February 2010, BRB, Bham (Elm). **Perf.** 2010: Bham (Elm)

Mozart Mass in C Minor (Page 146)
Music Wolfgang Amadeus Mozart; *Choreography* Oliver Hindle ('Credo' & 'Et incarnatus est'), David Justin ('Sanctus' & 'Benedictus'), Shimon Kalichman ('Qui tolis'& 'Benedictus'), Jillian Mackrill ('Kyrie'), Toby Norman-Wright ('Gratias'), Annette Pain ('Christe'), Jonathan Payn ('Gloria' & 'Benedictus'), Mikaela Polley ('Domine Deus' & 'Benedictus'), Nicole Tongue ('Laudamus te' & 'Benedictus'), Richard Whistler ('Quoniam'), Yuri Zhukov ('Jesu Christe' & 'Cum Sancto Spirito'); *Sets* Ian Preston *and* Heidi Öijar; *Costumes* Ian Preston, Heidi Öijar *and* Garry Jones; *Assistant Designer* Christian Doubble; *Lighting* Arnim Friess. **WP:** 2 May 1996, BRB, Bham. **Perf.** 1996: Bham

Much A-dance about Nothing
Music Igor Stravinsky; *Choreography* Jenny Murphy; *Designs* Lynsey Jackson; *Lighting* Nicholas Ware. **WP:** 2 June 2006, BRB, Bham. **Perf.** 2006: Bham

Piano Concerto in G
Music Maurice Ravel; *Choreography* Kit Holder; *Costumes* Sarah Burton; *Lighting* Johnny Westall-Eyre. **WP:** 11 February 2010, BRB, Bham (Elm). **Perf.** 2010: Bham (Elm)

Pictures at an Exhibition
Music Modest Mussorgsky; *Choreography* Shimon Kalichman ('The Old Castle'); Toby Norman-Wright ('Marketplace at Limoges' & 'Catacombs'); Annette Pain ('Samuel Goldenberg' & 'Shmuyle'); Jonathan Payn ('Tuileries' & 'Unhatched Chickens'); Mikaela Polley ('Cum mortuis in lingua mortua'); Samira Saidi ('Bydlo'); Nicole Tongue ('Baba-Yaga'); Asier Uriagereka ('Promenade'); Richard Whistler ('The Gnome'); Yuri Zhukov ('The Great Gate of Kiev'); *Designs* Laura O'Connell; *Assistant set designer* David Crisp; *Assistant costume designer* Michelle Longstaff; *Lighting* Nicholas Royle. **WP:** 29 May 1997, BRB, Bham. **Perf.** 1997: Bham

Planets, The (Page 148)
Music Gustav Holst; *Choreography* David Bintley ('Venus'); Samara Downs ('Mercury'); Kit Holder ('Uranus'); Rosie Kay ('Mars'); Michael Kopinski ('Saturn'); Jenny Murphy ('Neptune'); Lei Zhao ('Jupiter'); *Designs* Mark Simmonds; *Lighting* Peter Teigen *and* Nicholas Ware. **WP:** 15 June 2005, BRB, Bham. **Perf.** 2005: Bham

Plus de Sentiments
Music Astor Piazzolla; *Choreography* Kosuke Yamamoto; *Costumes* Claire Leadbeater *and* Kathrin Machno; *Lighting* Tim Leibe. **WP:** 27 May 2004, BRB, Bham (Pat). **Perf.** 2004: Bham (Pat)

Present Fears
Music Arvo Pärt; *Choreography* Alexander Whitley; *Costumes* Claire Leadbeater *and* Kathrin Machno; *Lighting* Steve Mackie. **WP:** 27 May 2004, BRB, Bham (Pat). **Perf.** 2004: Bham (Pat)

Printer Jam
Music Mistabishi; *Choreography* Kit Holder; *Costumes* Sarah Burton; *Lighting* Johnny Westall-Eyre. **WP:** 11 February 2010, BRB, Bham (Elm). **Perf.** 2010: Bham, Bham (CF), Bham (Elm)

Sequential Sextet
Music Antonín Dvořák; *Choreography* Jenny Murphy; *Costumes* Claire Leadbeater *and* Kathrin Machno; *Lighting* Tim Leibe. **WP:** 27 May 2004, BRB, Bham (Pat). **Perf.** 2004: Bham (Pat)

Shadow of my Son
Music Sergiu Pobereznic *and* Fergus Davidson; *Choreography* Sergiu Pobereznic; *Costumes* Claire Leadbeater *and* Kathrin Machno; *Lighting* Tim Leibe. **WP:** 27 May 2004, BRB, Bham (Pat). **Perf.** 2004: Bham (Pat)

Symphonic Dance
Music Sergei Rachmaninov; *Choreography* Kosuke Yamamoto; *Costumes* Claire Leadbeater *and* Kathrin Machno; *Lighting* Tim Leibe. **WP:** 27 May 2004, BRB, Bham (Pat). **Perf.** 2004: Bham (Pat)

Transitional Movement
Music Gustav Mahler; *Choreography* Samara Downs; *Lighting* Tim Leibe. **WP:** 27 May 2004, BRB, Bham (Pat). **Perf.** 2004: Bham (Pat)

Unfinished Sympathy
Music Arnold Bax; *Choreography* Michael Kopinski; *Costumes* Claire Leadbeater *and* Kathrin Machno; *Lighting* Steve Mackie. **WP:** 27 May 2004, BRB, Bham (Pat). **Perf.** 2004: Bham (Pat)

Unravelled (Page 144)
Music Igor Stravinsky; *Choreography* Nathanael Skelton; *Designs* Chloë Gamby; *Lighting* Nicholas Ware. **WP:** 2 June 2006, BRB, Bham. **Perf.** 2006: Bham

SPECIAL PERFORMANCES

20 Years Celebration (with guests)
The Orpheus Suite: opening; *The Nutcracker: Grand pas de deux; Concerto: pas de deux; Sylvia:* Pirates; *Carmina burana:* solo; *Hobson's Choice:* Will Mossop's Stag Night; *Romeo and Juliet:* Balcony *pas de deux; Slaughter on Tenth Avenue: pas de deux; Beauty and the Beast:* Act I *pas de deux; Printer Jam; Birthday Waltz; The Two Pigeons: pas de deux; Ballet Hoo!:* Mandolin Dance; *Aladdin:* Act II *pas de deux; Theme and Variations:* Polonaise. **Perf.** 2010: Bham

Conduct for Dance
Conducting competition open to a public audience and featuring *pas de deux* from *The Nutcracker, Swan Lake, The Sleeping Beauty* and *Le Corsaire*. **Perf.** 1993: Bham

Gala to Celebrate the Career of Desmond Kelly, A (with guests)
La Sylphide: Act II *pas de deux; Spring Waters pas de deux; Apollo: pas de deux; Prodigal Son: pas de deux; The Taming of the Shrew:* Fight *pas de deux; The Nutcracker: Grand pas de deux; Hobson's Choice:* Clog dance; *Enigma Variations:* Nimrod; *Ballet Hoo!:* Mandolin Dance; *Romeo and Juliet:* Balcony *pas de deux; Theme and Variations:* Polonaise. **Perf.** 2008: Bham

Silver Gala
The Seasons; Flowers of the Forest: Four Scottish Dances; *The Dance House: pas de deux; Hobson's Choice:* Lily of Laguna *pas de deux; Far from the Madding Crowd: Sword pas de deux; 'Still Life' at the Penguin Café.* **Perf.** 2001: Bham

Sir Fred and Mr B. Gala (with guests)
Tarantella; Monotones II; Concerto barocco: 3rd mvt; *Les Patineurs:* White *pas de deux* and *pas de trois; Agon: pas de deux; La Fille mal gardée:* Clog dance; *Five Brahms Waltzes in the Manner of Isadora Duncan; Slaughter on Tenth Avenue: pas de deux; Thaïs pas de deux; Façade:* Tango; *Cinderella:* Act II *pas de deux; Western Symphony:* 4th mvt. **Perf.** 2004: Bham

Sir Peter Wright Celebration Charity Gala (with Royal Ballet School students)
Serenade; Job: extracts; *Hornpipe, Sucitoarele, Valse fantaisie* (RBS); *Mirror Walkers: pas de deux; Romeo and Juliet:* Balcony *pas de deux; Hobson's Choice:* Lily of Laguna *pas de deux; Theme and Variations:* Polonaise; *Façade.* **Perf.** 1995: Bham